Before Maori

NZ's First Inhabitants

Ross M Bodle

www.createspace.com/3832110.
www.kindle.com

Copyright Ross M Bodle - December 2011

No part of this book may be copied in any form other than for the purposes of review.

This is a book that a layperson can read and gain from in understanding, embracing the true history of old and new *Aotearoa,* New Zealand.

Dedication:
To all the New Zealand born, we are one nation of diverse cultures, simply known as 'Kiwis' - a proud multicultural island nation in the far reaches of the Southern Pacific.

Contents:

Prologue p8

Chapter One: p11
Hawaiki, Maui, The Great Migration, Exploration & Discovery, Sample of a native fleet, Sea worthiness of Wakas, Did Maori sail to New Zealand or is it fantasy? Kaumatua, A Calabash sextant, Ships or canoes? Fortified settlements, Palisades in New Zealand, A parcel of lies, Value of hogs in the Pacific, Early man in New Zealand, Antarctica theory, Past Ice Ages, Stone age weapons, Greenstone (Pounamu).

Chapter Two: p35
Kumera plants (Ipomoea Batatas), The Manila Galleons, Celtic origins, Spanish navigation, Canoe voyages to Peru? Ships or canoes? Easter Island (Rapa Nui), Why not Maori? The mystery deepens, Heemerkirk & Zeehaen, Pre-Maori.

Chapter Three: p47
A dishonest act, Who really discovered New Zealand, Buried alive, Other small folk, The Australian Barrinean Pigmy, Pre-Maori historical sites, Secretive digs, Lake Taupo volcanic eruption 186AD, Further evidence, Headstone, Factual findings 1860, Modern findings 2009, Patupaiarehe inhabitants.

Chapter Four: p63
The International road show, Juan Fernandez, Taniwha dragon, Kiore black rat, The Moa Hunters, Native dogs (Kuri), Massive earthquake,

Oldest record of man in New Zealand, Headstone, Musket tribal wars, The three main reasons for the treaty.

<u>Chapter Five: p74</u>
Genealogy/Whakapapa, The Ancient of Days, Let my people go, Shepherd Kings, Christian Education in New Zealand, Aramaic/Semitic language, New update, hawk (Kahu), who are the True Indigenous People of New Zealand?

<u>Chapter Six: p87</u>
The first People, Moriori, Waitaha (Children of Maui), Our Cultural Future, Maori today, Toronto, Utu/revenge/payback, A Nation Under Siege, Apartheid/segregation, A Massive Cover Up, Your Cooperation is required, Herea Te tangata ki Te whenua (Binding people to the land).

<u>Chapter Seven:</u> p99
Wake up New Zealand, A country that's divided will fall, A National Day of Prayer, Incident # One, Incident # Two, A Non Win Situation, Epilogue, A Spiritual Awareness, New Zealand's National Anthem, Bibliography, References & Further Reading, Post Script, The Challenge, A Manual for all mankind

Bibliography p112

Preface:
For sixty odd years I've listened to our cultural problems some of which been caused by deception or misunderstanding by *Pakeha* (Europeans) and *Maori* alike. Moreover, I'm deeply disappointed in our politicians making these so called settlements payments and foreshore rights agreements to *iwi* (tribes) without checking the ground work first. The main reason I've put this essay together is so that the truth can be exposed and viewed by all cultures wherever as to who are the true indgenous people of *Aotearoa,* New Zealand. Politicians need to understand that the past generations of Maori landowners were ready and willing to sell flax, tattooed heads, and land to obtain weapons for an *'Utu'* (revenge) and the early New Zealand Polynesian as a race were obviously not the first settlers to *Aotearoa* as they claim, and the modern Pakeha-Maori are reaping the benefits, *why?*

'The greater the lie, the more likely it is to be believed.' Hitler's Minister *of Propaganda,* Josef Goebbels.

About the Author:
I'm a New Zealander and an ardent one at that being from *'Ngati Porou'* on the East Coast of the North Island. At an early age we as a family found our local Maori a proud fun loving people who gave many hours of education and encouragement in the way of Maoridom. This I've personally cherished as taught through 'Mary Grey' our adorable Maori nanny from 'Tokomaru Bay' an *iwi* (tribe) known for its knowledge on healing properties. The area mentioned above is situated near the modern city of Gisborne on the North Island of New Zealand. *(Ngati - descendents of).*

Introduction:

Throughout the years we have visited museums around the Pacific and found evidence that left us wondering about the identity of our earlier cultures. Some research material gave detailed descriptions of extraordinary discoveries, some findings were pretentious, but are included here so that readers can evaluate it and draws their own conclusions. Part of the material collected seems incredible, perhaps offensive; it's the truth as we have found it and this book is our heartfelt effort to share it with you in the best way possible. Moreover, the theories and controversies surrounding Polynesia still grow daily. We are still researching, delving into whatever, whenever, in other words it's ongoing...

In each country visited we have talked to a learned few on the above subject, as my wife Sylvia and I are interested in the anthropology of the Pacific people, and what better way than using our sailboat as a vehicle to do this whilst sailing around these colourful islands?

What is anthropology?

Basically, it's a study of mankind, a group of sciences all rolled into one mostly covering the following subjects; field work in all that it contains, cultural development, doctrines, origin, social, languages, archaeology, kinship and mythology to just name a few. It usually involves a combination of many people, universities, especially government funding, research that can't be rushed; it takes time and a huge amount of capital.

Our own research has been difficult, as we are not supported by outside means being totally independent. Now I have a partner, my wife finds the research interesting and somewhat challenging despite the hardships involved. Obviously some of the verbal material passed on to me over the past sixty years is backed up from the extracts enclosed, as the writer has allowed enough snippets to get the reader's attention on specific subjects without harming cultures. Furthermore, you can follow up our research material by contacting your local archives or using the Amazon website. www.amazon.com/books

Prologue

The manuscript below is a compilation of documents, newspaper articles of so-called expert opinion about pre-Maori and Maori occupation of New Zealand. Many a passive Maori has come forward questioning their history that has been presented to them by influential people, academics, both Maori and *Pakeha* (European) as many believe they are descendants of a very ancient civilization that once inhabited New Zealand long before the arrival of Maori; some *iwi* (tribe) called them the *'forest that whisperers,'* whilst others made out that they were just a myth or a legend and were not real people at all but ghosts, they were called by Maori the *Waitaha,* a forest dwelling people. Also enclosed are the findings and tales that have been handed down amongst *iwi* about fair skinned people and the deliberate determined effort by some to squash the legitimacy of these ancient tribes. Some *iwi* tribes have declared it as *tapu,* forbidden, to talk about them, whilst other Maori as settlers tell of another culture called the *Patu-pai-arehe,* recorded from their own voyages, believing that there was more than one race living in New Zealand long before the coming of Maori.

<u>*A conspiracy*</u>?

The book by Michael King on early New Zealand history, used as gospel amongst academics, politicians and influential people, is now under the spotlight as there are too many anomalies discovered by other historians from archaeological finds. It is this anomaly that has created a conspiracy theory that was reinforced when police were alleged to have stated that; *'the death of Michael King and his wife in a car wreck was at the time suspicious.'*

The massive cover up:
Due to the *Waitangi Tribunal* many pre-Maori artifacts found by Europeans or Maori in Northland have been handed over to local *iwi* called the *Te Roroa Hapu, 'Waipoua Advisory Committee Authority'* as pre-Maori bones and other archaeological finds as evidence are removed from the site then either kept, buried or deliberately destroyed. *Why?*

It's our heritage:
Hopefully, at some stage in the future many of our passive Maori with alleged *Patu-pai-arehe* and *Waitaha* blood will have the opportunity to make sure that these items will be protected so they too can actually touch, look, ponder, and marvel at such things that their ancestors had once used.

National Security:
The driving force behind this essay is in support of those underprivileged few who believe they have the DNA of the ancient *Maru-iwi*, *Waitaha* or the *Patu-paiarehe,* and their need to uncover the reason for the fourteen pages of alleged carbon dating of archeological evidence which has been restricted from public view until 2063 on the grounds of National Security. *Why?*

A renewed beginning:
The following information will be of a brief nature only as some of it will surprise you and perhaps enlighten especially our native brothers and sisters, but you have to follow through by checking out the facts yourself. The reader will need pen and paper to make notes as I've included websites to give access to material one usually cannot find published elsewhere; also details of books numbered accordingly at the end of these chapters. Please note; I've deliberately left out page numbers, as the reader regardless of educational merit will never be

able to grasp the real significant meaning to Maoridom by just reading a few lines, especially on a specific subject. Have a good read then do your research; whatever your findings, you will certainly find it awe-inspiring.

Chapter One:

Hawaiki, Maui, The Great Migration, Exploration & Discovery, Sample of a native fleet, Sea worthiness of Wakas, Did Maori sail to New Zealand or is it fantasy? Kaumatua, A Calabash sextant, Ships or canoes? Fortified settlements, Palisades in New Zealand, Landed Aliens from the west, The name of Maori, A parcel of lies, Value of hogs in the Pacific, Early man in New Zealand, Antarctica theory, Past Ice Ages, Stone age weapons, Greenstone (Pounamu).

Please Note:
In the following comments I want to make very, very clear we are not taking sides, putting down Maori or being in anyway racist, nor is it designed to create disunity as we respect and admire their differences in custom and culture. This essay is designed to help the reader to investigate for themselves the real history of New Zealand, as the truth must be told and passed on as recorded by those famous few within Maoridom who had the knowledge and wisdom now recorded below.

Hawaiki: (Distant home 1350 BCE).
I suffer from a great disadvantage as there have been others before me who already compiled an excellent presentation of the early history of *Aotearoa* (New Zealand), however it seems not all about the Pacific inhabitants have been mentioned - perhaps their personal history doesn't blend in with what some academics require or like other information has been distorted, or suppressed?
There has to be a starting point as where the Pacific people came from, to do this one has to trace their origins; when asked all in turn mentioned a far-off place called *'Hawaiki.'* This name derives from

Polynesian belief that refers to an island in the Cook Group somewhere near Rarotonga, whilst others arguably believe it to be in the Marquesas (*Hiva Oa*) in French Polynesia, often referred as the 'Hub' of Polynesia? In fact ancient script suggests otherwise as *Hawaiki* isn't an island but a distant home far removed from the South Pacific.

Maui:
According to Maori Mythology, the largest Pacific Island landmass *Aotearoa* New Zealand was fished out of the sea by a demi-god called *Maui* who supernaturally achieved the impossible. A supernatural being or spiritual presence as told throughout Polynesia; it was this same *Maui* who founded their islands and atolls simply by hauling fishing lines from his *Vaka* canoe, a much occupied demi-god.

The Great Migration:
The arrival of seven canoes en masse to '*Aotearoa*' (New Zealand) simultaneously is simply a myth, as the voyages would have been occurring at intervals taking several weeks, months or perhaps generations. For example, when a racing fleet of sailboats leave New Zealand waters for the Fijian Islands, all carry satellite navigation (GPS), chart plotters that give course, speed over ground, and ship's position to within a few metres. Even with the ultimate equipment installed and crew expertise, they still cannot manage to arrive at the required destination together, it is simply not possible. To be realistic, the migrating *Vakas* (canoes) would have been spread out after the first canoe departed, as storms and gales would have separated the fleet with some vessels being lost at sea. Moreover, making a voyage from eastern Polynesia for a distance of over four thousand miles, to actually sail directly to an unknown land without some prior knowledge beforehand, is simply folly. One can only presume that there had been sightings of volcanic activity plumes from Taupo, (186 AD), and the volcanoes of Ruapehu, Egmont/Taranaki and Rangitoto (500AD.) '*Bloody*

sky' etc, as most would have been active around that period. Also perhaps smoke from the massive bush fires created by the volcanoes gave the approximate position of *Aotearoa?* 32, 44.

Exploration & Discovery:
After the cyclone season had finished (November-April), each *Vaka* crew loaded enough supplies for approximately two weeks and left their home islands, sailing into fresh southeast trade-wind always shunting the mainsail, tacking in a zigzag pattern whilst each navigator studied the heavens, swell movements above and below the surface as well as bird life for tell-tale signs of approaching land. When nearly depleted of supplies and with no islands in sight, each canoe returned to their home running before the trades - that's how it was done.

Worthy of note:
The nearest alien island northwest of *Aotearoa* (New Zealand) is New Caledonia with a *Vaka* sailing time frame of 10-12 days depending on trade-wind strength. *Melanesian culture # one.*

Kupe & Toi:
Whilst visiting other island groups one had learned of such a land to the south. With this knowledge *Kupe* in 925AD made an exploratory voyage southwards, presumably from Tahiti, leaving probably from Melanesia or perhaps Fiji. Using an *'Ndrua'* or Tongan *'Kalia'* known as a fast ocean-sailing outrigger (proa) canoes, he found *Aotearoa* New Zealand to be uninhabited and returned to confirm their findings.

Once this was carried out, more canoes *Toi* (the wood eater) in *(1150 - 1350 AD)* and others would have left in stages as time and seasons allowed. This latter theory was confirmed by the late Dr David Lewis (who has written many a paper and books on this specific subject) whilst the author attended a dinner evening in Whitianga in the Bay of Plenty.

I caught up with David again at the Auckland Maritime Museum and knowing of my interest in anthropology he asked me to join him on a voyage to Rarotonga. It would have been a fabulous experience but I had to decline his kind offer due to commitments. 48, 51, 52. (*See Obituary online; Dr David Lewis, under New Zealand Archaeology*).

<u>Sample of a Native Naval Fleet:</u>
It's interesting to note the show of strength when warring parties got together as witnessed by Captain James Cook, Foster and Hodges when visiting 'King George Island' *(Tahiti*) in 1774, as they observed a fleet of 160 double hulled warships in *'Pare Bay'*, some with fighting platforms, plus another 170 smaller canoe-type sailing craft with approximately 7-8000 warriors preparing for an attack on the neighbouring island of Moorea. Each *Vaka* carried 40 rowers/paddlers armed with spears, clubs and stones for slings.

Dr David Lewis, Ross, Marge and Mike Phear

Cook mentioned a fleet of ships; if this holds true then these vessels would have been massive, large enough to carry freight/cargo to be used as a type of transport carrying many warriors. The smaller faster vessels (proa) out-riggers commandeered supplies to Moorea and if applicable the wounded and deceased back to Tahiti. 48.

Worthy of note:
Vaka is the Polynesian word for canoe whilst *Waka* is the same for Maori.

Sea worthiness of Wakas:
Whilst on the subject of sailing vessels, an item on 'CNN News' showed a large Maori *Waka* capsize in the waves off the harbour entrance thus giving the characteristics of a mono-hulled canoe. This took place during the 'Millennium Bicentenary New Year 2000' at Gisborne on the East Coast noted to be the first city on our planet to receive the sun. However, the larger double *Waka/Vaka* (catamaran) joined with lashed beams were compatible with the movement of the sea.

Did Maori sail to New Zealand or is it fantasy?
I've asked many local Maori around Northland this particular question with a deliberate selection of age group between 20-40 years. *"Do you believe that your ancestors actually sailed to New Zealand from the Pacific Islands?"* Their individual answers are as follows;

(a) "No way, we have always been here."

(b) "We came in one large canoe bringing with us animals, plants and over 1000 people at a time."

(c) "We came on the early whaling ships and not in canoes."

(d) "Yes, we must have because we are here aren't we, bro?"

(e) "We found Aotearoa by accident after a fishing canoe got lost and drifted from the islands."

(f) "I'm not sure? I personally feel that it's not possible for frail canoes to venture that far without having the proper navigation skills and adequate food supplies."

Nevertheless, regardless of the debates involving Polynesian ocean passages, our personal findings tell us voyages did actually take place using their double hulled 60-70 ft ocean-going canoes *Nga Waka O Nehera.* To enable such voyages each had to be planned well in advance to survive the vast distances, however, if the native population was found to be under threat and forced to leave quickly, their vessels in whatever shape or form would have been poorly equipped. As to a lost fishing party or drift voyage to New Zealand under the same circumstances, as one young so-called *Kaumatua* firmly believed, it is simply folly, as one cannot sustain long periods at sea without water for more than seven or eight days especially in open vessels. One must remember that New Zealand is far removed from the prevailing easterly trade wind usually found at approximately 25 degrees latitude.

<u>*Worthy of note:*</u>
The role of a *Kaumatua* in Maoridom is that one has to be male, exceptionally chosen by his tribe, to act as a spoke person on the marae, to be a keeper of knowledge in the traditions of the I*wi Hapu* (sub-tribe) and is actively involved with his *Whanau* (extended family) as a respected elder.

Calabash sextant:

The following newspaper clipping of such a voyage will help clear disbeliefs; also to enlighten the reader. Taken from 'The Evening Post 29th March, 1926.' (Page 10):

'Maori Navigators Regular Ocean Voyages. A Calabash Sextant, Admiral Rodman Inquires.'

Throughout the Pacific Islands tradition is abundant that the Polynesians did actually voyage, of deliberate design, across long ocean stretches. Captain J. Bollons, of the Government steamer Tutanekai, while admitting that the ancestors of the Maori came to New Zealand by canoe, contends that they were victims of circumstances, and were driven offshore by adverse weather. In an article in the "Auckland Star," Mr Frank Bodle states that the Admiral Rodman (who accompanied the United States fleet which recently visited New Zealand as a guest), compared notes on the subject of Maori migration with Dr P.H. Buck. Admiral Rodman stated that when he was in command of the Hawaiian naval station about 1906, he was informed by the natives that in the former days, and at regular intervals, a fleet of Hawaiian canoes set out from those islands, steering by the stars, for Tahiti and the island of Raiatia. On the latter island there was a famous marae, regarded as so sacred by Polynesians that natives from distant islands voyaged thereto in order to take away a stone as the nucleus for an altar in any new settlement. On the island of Raiatia high mysteries were celebrated. The Admiral was sceptical as to the navigating powers of the islanders, but the natives were emphatic and recited the old sailing directions. They explained that the traverse to Tahiti was without serious difficulty but, owing to adverse winds and currents, the return voyage requires great skill. On the homeward journey it was necessary to take what sailors would call the starboard tack, steering far to the eastward of Hawaii, crossing the Line well out towards the American Continent.

Again the admiral professed profound scepticism, and the natives, piqued by this, which they called "the magic calabash." When the northern constellation, which we call the Little Bear, was sighted, said the natives, the calabash was brought into use. This curious nautical instrument had four holes in its circumference, forming a level line. The bowl was filled with water to the level of the holes, and the native observer sighted through a back hole over the far rim at Polaris, the Pole star, exactly as a modern sailor might do with modern instruments. When satisfied of their position the fleet turned due west and invariably made home. This Admiral, still dubious, experimented himself, and found by careful measurement that the angle used by the old navigators was 19 degrees – and Hawaii is 19 degrees north of the Equator. Quite evidently these Hawaiians found the latitude of Hawaii when many hundreds of miles away, and sailed down to their home, correcting their position each evening by fresh sights. For the purpose of these Polynesians, said the Admiral to Dr Buck, this magical calabash was efficient and accurate an instrument as those used by seamen of today. Admiral Rodman made searching inquiries, and in discussing the whole matter in a Honolulu paper, recorded his conviction that the Hawaiians definitely and regularly voyaged from Hawaii to Tahiti and back.

So far as the Maori voyage to New Zealand is concerned, states Mr F. H. Bodle, there is no suggestion of anything like the magical calabash, but the story of the Maori migration, preserved throughout New Zealand, is supported by linking genealogies in Tahiti and this country, by various island food plants transported to an acclimatized New Zealand – drift canoes would inevitably exhaust their food supplies are reachable here, leaving nothing to plant – and by evidence of the stars. The sailing directions for the original fleet have been preserved, and they refer to various stars as guides. These enumerated stars would be quite useless for the voyage today, but careful calculations have shown that their positions in the heavens 500 to 600 years ago – the migration period according to genealogies – these stars would be accurate guides for the journey to New Zealand. All the evidence tends to confirm the detailed traditions of Tahiti and of New Zealand.

The seamanship of the Polynesians and the sea worthiness of their craft are admitted by Captain Bollons, while their skilled navigators is attested by many acute observers, amongst whom Captain Cook and Admiral Rodman testify as experts.

The book on "Maori Canoes and Canoes of the Pacific Islands" published by Mr Elsdon Best, a recognized authority on Polynesian history, contains a map which shows that according to tradition, numerous voyages were made between the groups of islands.' 52. <u>End Quote.</u> (Online).

The Polynesians were great seamen who were skilled at the ancient art of building what some would call primitive fragile sailing vessels that were fast and light in construction. Some hold the view that they were hundreds of years ahead of their European counterparts, the same applied to their navigation methods and their incredible knowledge of the stars. 28, 29, 46, 48.

<u>Ships or Canoes?</u>
To prepare for such a voyage to New Zealand each *Vaka* carried coconuts, gourds, and bamboo poles filled with water; this feat certainly seems feasible, but while carrying cargo and a large crew, the idea of towing coconut fiber lines with mussels attached whilst the crew held a large basket (*kete*) fixed between the hulls for food and bait would have to be another fable as one would expect that having all that extra weight plus drag would slow and swamp a voyaging canoe.

However, our personal research tells that a seventy foot multi-hull *Vaka* held a crew of 175 souls; both hulls had 84 paddlers in each section and another seven to hold the *kete* basket with the crew being a mix of men and women; the latter especially chosen for breeding. The crew caught fish while in transit allowing the flesh to be eaten raw, having juices instead of drinking fresh water. They shared four great 21ft steering sweeps; if the latter holds true then these vessels were not canoes but ships. As mentioned above, the early pre-Maori native settlers tell of crews paddling to a set of drums. The latter is confusing because one can't paddle large ships; perhaps both large and smaller vessels were used in transit?

Captain Cook's thoughts at that time; *'they cannot remain at sea above two weeks as water and food supply would be depleted by then.'* 4, 48.

Fortified settlements:
It's interesting to note that when European explorers first charted the Pacific there had been discoveries of large defence systems in the form of upright wooden posts 12 ft above ground, used to protect villages throughout Melanesian Papua New Guinea. Some were situated in the highlands whilst others were located in the surrounding islands, with some found on level ground enclosing village settlements. The latter fortresses had water filled moats on the outer rim for protection. The same had been found in the high hills of *Aotearoa* (New Zealand) but I personally have yet to see one with a moat. However, I've since learnt of one small ancient 'Pa-site' with a moat-post-palisade fortification that had been located in the Waikato district, now gone due to natural forces over a period of time. The palisades at former times were numerous in *Aotearoa* New Zealand but little known in Polynesia; since Maori migrated from the eastern region of the Pacific it suggests that they had adopted a system from another culture. 1, 2.

Worthy of note:
In level ground villages around Melanesia there were palisades surrounded by 6-9ft earthworks with moats outside, some having two or three moats and earthen mounds in between. Each was well fortified, with muddy water at waist height having fire-hardened sharpened

stakes of split bamboo well placed below the surface, and trip lines/vines to catch the unwary. The pathway across consisted of two logs so placed that only one man could cross at a time, and above each palisade entrance a projecting platform was guarded by warriors who threw spears/darts, shot arrows, and threw down large stones, also using slings. Some fortifications were surrounded by a maze of ditches large enough to literally get lost in. 52. *(Melanesian custom # two).*

Palisades in New Zealand:
Here we have two different cultures, Melanesian and Polynesian-Maori, separated by thousands of miles of ocean but they have the same defences. It seems incredible, so how come? This question will be answered shortly but first let's take a look at what early European explorers had to say on this topic. It seems that the native Polynesian didn't introduce palisades to *Aotearoa* (New Zealand) as quoted from Captain James Cook's log whilst he was in 'Bora Bora,' a Polynesian Island group.

'The crew from HMS Discovery and HMS Resolution witnessed a mock battle given by the Polynesian natives to demonstrate their effectiveness in their naval strategy. For the safety of these islands each community relied upon its navy of war canoes, never fighting on land only on the water accustomed are they from birth to the sea and the maneuvering of their vessels. Each war canoe measured between 60-70 ft in length and had fighting platforms mounted aboard for warriors to fight on.'

Cook was suitably impressed and rated that it could be a learning curve using these same tactics for the British Admiralty.

One must remember that the atolls and islands around the eastern Pacific have coral reefs as a natural barrier for protection surrounding each island thus having lagoons; it was here that battles were fought either outside the reef or in calmer waters but never fighting on land. Joseph Banks, also from Cook's ship, reported in his writings the same with an additional mention about *Vaka* fighting platforms and natives often ramming canoes.

Worthy of note:
In New Zealand the palisades, corner posts and centre post of large meeting houses around *'ancient Pa sites'* had human remains at the base, each located in a sitting position embracing the posts. These have been found in the Bay of Plenty, especially around *Maketu* between *Tauranga* and *Whakatane*, also on the delta area of the Opotiki and Motu Rivers. The same could be found along the *Urenui River,* twenty miles northeast of New Plymouth on the West Coast of the North Island such as *Maru-whi, Poho-kura, Okoki,* ancient Pa hill sites that had been occupied long before the arrival of Maori. The dark skinned *Maru-iwi* people as named by Maori are believed to be of Melanesian descent, having come from a warmer climate, as they had bushy/frizzy hair like Fijians. They were a tall slim race with very dark skin and were big boned with flat facial features. Their slaves unfortunately were forced to hold the posts upright whilst they were buried alive, definitely not a Maori custom.

The *Maru-iwi* inhabited most of the North Island upon the arrival of 'Toi' in the first emigrational canoe as found in Northland, Hokianga, Tamaki, Hauraki, Taranaki, Urewera National Park, Opotiki, Mohaka, Te Wairoa, Taupo, Mokau, Nuhaka, and other locations. The palisades and defense systems had to be adopted from these earlier people *(Tanga Whenua)*. 1, 2, 52. Melanesian custom # three.

Evening Post 31st July 1917, page 9. Reference; Wellington Harbour.
"   "   "   15th July 1930, page 3. Reference; Moriori & Maori.
"   "   "   2nd May 1918, page 3. Reference; Rock paintings. (*Online*).

The references above mention that *Kupe* and *Ngahue* sighted *Aotearoa* New Zealand after sailing from Tahiti in two canoes called *Mata-horua* and the *Tawari-rangi*. The following conflicting reports are confusing.

(a). Mentions that *Kupe* and *Ngahue* sailed from the North Cape down the East Coast and into Wellington Harbour then traversed the west coast of the South island and found moa bones and some greenstone before returning to their home island.

(b). Also states that the canoes circumnavigated the whole of New Zealand with no mention of finding a moa bone or greenstone, only citing that Aotearoa was uninhabited.

(c). That Kupe sailed with his wife and two daughters in one canoe carrying 300 people traveling from *Tahiti* to cross the great ocean *Moana-nui-a-Kiwi* to Castle Point on the Wairarapa Coast and settled before heading down to the South Island.

(d). After a portage across Auckland hinterland the two 60ft double hulled Vakas of approximately 25 tons each sailed down the west coast to Taranaki.

Factual report and evidence states that Kupe made landfall on the Wairarapa Coast near Castle Point before heading south into the Wellington Harbour, naming the two islands within after his daughters before heading down the west coast of the South Island. 52.

Landed Aliens from the west:
The *Maru-iwi* arrived in three canoes, and they landed on Taranaki's west coast and settled in the Urenui district. They came from a tropical land called *Papa-nui-a-tau* to the west; presumed to be the *Moriori* who were of Melanesian stock. Moreover, Maori described these dark

skinned folk as being repulsive, having bushy hair, rude habits and being very susceptible to cold, a treacherous people.

Approximately three hundred years later the arrival of 'Toi' from the island of *Samoa* brought people who settled in the Bay of Plenty and bred with the local inhabitants, thus starting a new breed of mixed cultures. The *Maru-iwi/Moriori* believed to be the first people to settle *Aotearoa* New Zealand, having landed at *Nga Motu 'The Sugar Loaf Islets'* making their fortified villages/Pa hill sites along the banks of the Urenui River. 52.

Name of Maori:

The people of the Pacific were usually named after the islands they came from for example; *Hawaiian, Tongan, Fijian, Samoan, Tahitian or Nui* Islander but coming from *Aotearoa* (New Zealand) one would think they would have been called an *Aotearoan* native? Regardless of what people may believe, the actual native Polynesian Maori had no name for themselves, having only tribal names such as *'Tangata Maori'* meaning ordinary people, descendants of what is presumed to be the country's first Polynesian immigrants. Nevertheless, with the arrival of Europeans the word 'MAORI' gradually became the adjective, this change took place before 1815. *(Source: New Zealand Encyclopedia, 4th Edition Bateman).*

Captain Cook:

Whilst on the subject of Captain James Cook, it's worth mentioning that 'Cook' did not discover New Zealand nor did the Dutch or Spanish as taught in schools and stated in history books. There is however written evidence that the British Admiralty handed Cook some Portuguese charts of the Southern Ocean with New Zealand and Australia already printed on them. These charts were put together by a Turkish Admiral *Piri Reis* and showed the northern and southern pack ice limits, even gave evidence to the Americas on both coasts from the north and down to include the *Straits of Magellan, Tierra del Fuego and Cape Horn* in the south plus the *Falklands, South Georgia, Auckland, and South Shetland Islands* including *New Zealand* and *Australia*.

The British Admiralty commanded Cook to claim New Zealand and Australia for England, which he did in 1769 & 1770. Moreover, the *'Piri Reis Charts'* were dated in 1422-3, that's 98 years before Magellan (1520), 220 years before Abel Tasman (1642), 347 years before Cook's arrival in the south Pacific (1769) and 70 years before Christopher Columbus's discovery of the Americas (1492). All Cook had to do was to sail southward from *Tahiti* to reach latitude 37 - 38 degrees south then set a course westward (longitude hadn't been discovered until Cook's second voyage) to New Zealand, landing in Poverty Bay on the east coast on the 9th of October 1769, knowing that sooner or later he would reach land. The same applied when sailing towards Australia in (1770). 6. (Some historians have dated the Poverty Bay landing as the 6th October 1769).

Worthy of note:
Admiral Piri Reis wasn't the cartographer of these charts; they were either pirated, or purchased at a great price by the British Admiralty, as charts were jealously guarded and held in secret locations by their respected navies. If this holds true, who were the original cartographers? *(Piri Reis, Harleian & Rotz charts, online).*

Parcel of lies:
Tupia, a native 'High Priest Navigator' from the island of *Raiatea,* accompanied Cook on *HMS. Endeavour.* He had shown where all the surrounding islands were situated including *Aotearoa* New Zealand. Joseph Banks overheard *Tupia* questioning East Coast Maori boasting of their return trips to the islands - he called them *'a parcel of liars'* as no

Rangatira (chieftain) would allow a trip from the islands without bringing back hogs. 1, 2, 3, 6, 9, 20, 27, 35, 45, 48.

Value of hogs in the Pacific:
Even today the Pacific Island natives can purchase a wife just for one pig and two axes, as hogs to the Melanesian native are a sign of wealth that can be used as barter or in paying back a debt. Animals are rare in the Pacific and pigs are valuable to natives but they will provide one for special occasions, to be eaten only by the menfolk. One must remember that due to the shortage of fresh meat the Melanesian and Maori native turned to cannibalism, their acceptance to bury the dead after a battle was a sheer waste of flesh and they preferred to consume them; this practice however was rare in Polynesia. 48. *(Melanesian custom # four)*

In fourteen hundred and ninety two
Columbus sailed the ocean blue
With maps in hand drawn before
He headed straight for Cuba's shore
Much fame he gained, so I'm told
For he proved true the maps of old.

Early man in New Zealand:
History and DNA samples tell us that a race of people migrated from Austroasia (Taiwan), an island nation off the east coast of mainland China, sailed either side of the equator allowing for trade winds depending on the seasons, moved from island to island where they mixed, bred and adopted customs. If they found them hostile, they avoided or overcame them then settled until over-population forced them to move on. This we feel is the obvious route taken as the Melanesians in New Caledonia, Vanuatu, Fiji and Kingdom of Tonga show Polynesian/European facial features and in some cases lighter skin

colouring, a sure sign of mix-breeding. Nevertheless, some academics hold the view the early Polynesians left by foot or surface craft, perhaps both, to follow the Asian coastal route around the northern western Pacific to cross the Bering Sea, going down the Alaskan coast using the prevailing winds and tides to reach the Western Coastal regions of present-day Canada and United States, with the odd vessel calling in on the local inhabitants (Amerindians) before re-entering the Pacific from the east. Historians hold the view that the Polynesians had traversed as far afield as Hawaii in the north, Easter Island, the Americas in the east, Madagascar in the Indian Ocean to the west, southwest to New Zealand, then further southward to the sub-Antarctic Auckland Islands. (More on this later).

The Antarctica theory:
Due to pole shifts (the modern term for global warming) parts of the Bering Sea; the *Arctic* landscape and *Antarctica* continents were free of ice, allowing northern Alaska and *'Terra Del Fuego'* (Chile) in South America to be populated at approximately the same time. One must remember that the present Arctic and Antarctic regions at one stage had been forests, with a warm climate that allowed habitation of wildlife. Nevertheless, some scholars now presume that a group of people actually migrated in an easterly direction; they had food, shelter and would breed whilst on the move as did the Bering Strait Inuit/Eskimo. The latter natives proved beyond doubt that this type of inhabitation is certainly feasible; it is this theory of migration to Australia, New Zealand, and South America from Africa that's actually taught in Chilean schools, along with the Bering Sea crossing in the Northern hemisphere. 8. *(Pole-shifts & the Chander wobble, online).*

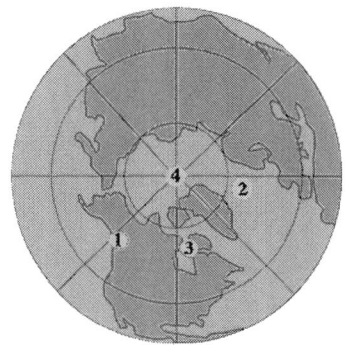

Past Ice Ages: View: 'Google Map'.

Just to give the reader an idea of different locations in regards to actual 'Poles' during the past ice ages I've allowed navigational waypoints Wpts, (fixes) to follow up on.

(1) 63 degrees north 135 degrees west approximately (80,000 BP), centred East of Anchorage, Alaska, USA.

(2) 72 degrees north 10 degrees east approximately (50 - 55,000 BP), centred Northeast of Oslo, Norway.

(3) 60 degrees north 73 degrees west approximately (12 - 17,000 BP), centred in Hudson Bay, in the northern Quebec, Ontario and Manitoba Provinces of Canada.

(4) Present location created approximately (2010 BP). (BP Before present). *Online.*

If we place the same latitude in the Southern Hemisphere whilst using the opposite longitude positions from the above we would find the South Pole ice mass extending well into the Indian, Pacific and Atlantic Oceans, for example:

(1) 63 degrees south 135 degrees east, the South Pole centred below Adelaide in South Australia north of the present Antarctica, having ice-floes/bergs off and around the Island of Tasmania, and the southwest portion of New Zealand to also include the Indian Ocean.

(2) 72 degrees south 10 degrees west situated approximately half way between Africa and the South American continents allowing ice-floes/bergs to cover a larger southern portion of the Atlantic.

(3) 60 degrees south 73 degrees east, situated just below the Kerguelen Island group with the ice- floes/bergs scattered halfway between Africa and Western Australian continents.

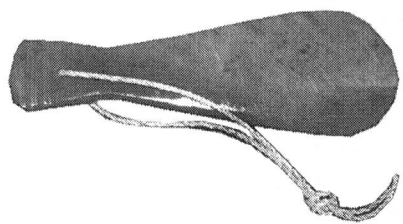

Stone age weaponry:
I've previously mentioned Americas and Asia for good reason to back up our research, due to an amazing discovery of artifacts uncovered last century of greenstone *'Hei tikis'* and a *mere,* the latter being a club used for hand-to-hand combat by Maori warriors. These were found in Chile on the west coast of South America. How the *'greenstone mere'* and *'Hei Tikis'* came to Chile remains a mystery - perhaps they came from a Spanish Galleon or a 'spouter' (slang term for whaling ships)?
Our research shows that *'tikis'* (a Demigod for Polynesians) and the *patu* and the *mere* are not original to the Pacific as first believed, as they have also been found in Europe, Palestine, Israel including Egypt Asia and Mexico. 2, 33. *(Origins of the Haka & Bes – Tiki online).*

Greenstone (Pounamu):

Let's take a look at the type of materials used to make these artifacts. The Polynesian *'Hei Tikis'* and the *'mere'* (club) are carved objects, usually made from whalebone or fire hardened wood, materials that are available anywhere around the oceans of the world. But to have it made from greenstone which is similar to jade can be confusing as it's a totally different material altogether.

Jade can be found in Asia, Europe, and Central America as elsewhere but to the native Maori, greenstone is only found in New Zealand. Let's see what the Oxford Dictionary says on this topic.

<u>Jadeite:</u>
A semiprecious stone, varying in colour from deep green through to yellow, brown and white

<u>Use</u>: *ornaments, jewelry.*

<u>Greenstone / Nephrite:</u>
A dark green igneous extremely hardened rock containing minerals feldspar and hornblend. Formerly molten; describes rock formed under conditions of intense heat or produced by solidifications of volcanic magma on or below the Earth.

<u>Use:</u> *Maori weapons, ceremonial axes and jewelry.*

The only locality where excellent nephrite can be obtained is in rivers and creeks near Hokitika in the South island and Queenstown. The sort after stone almost emerald-green in colour is scarce and hard to find with a hardness of 6.5 it cannot chip; only be cut by using a diamond a hardness scale of 10.

There is however a green softer type stone that's used for carving of jewelry or weapons even to the extent of using coloured glass-hardened-resin shaped Hei-Tikis an imitation of the real thing, a real tourist trap.

A mistaken identity of jade or greenstone as such is a huge disappointment for collectors, especially in the case of a stone pigeon 'Korotangi,' unearthed around the 1880s between Raglan and Kawhia in the Waikato district, which was thought to be greenstone material but later found to be of only green serpentine nephrite. The stone serpentine bird in question is believed to have come from an Indonesian source from an Arabian *dhow,* a sailing ship used by Arabs during the late eighteenth century.

When at sea in overcast conditions sailing ships were often lost, sometimes for weeks, with no sun sights. It was then that pigeons were released and these would fly off to the nearest land. A magical experience for sailors who found it difficult to understand a bird that can navigate without instruments let alone flight, to be admired, even worshipped, and the reason why such carvings were often carried on board dhows. If the above bird is truly made from serpentine/jade material then the Waikato Maori Royal Family whom I've been informed have this particular artifact in their possession could now have an embarrassing situation. *(View: Arabs explorers 790 AD online).*

Chapter Two:

Kumara plants (Ipomoea Batatas), The Manila Galleons, Celtic origins, Spanish navigation, Canoe voyages to Peru? Ships or canoes? Easter Island (Rapa Nui), Why not Maori? The mystery deepens, Heemerkirk & Zeehaen, Pre-Maori.

The kumara plants: (Ipomoea batatas)
Kumara then would have been a little larger than finger size; almost black in colour (not the modern large hybrid tubers of today). They could be found throughout the Pacific Islands and are believed to have come from Northern Peru in South America. We find it interesting that ocean passages were made often, suggesting a source of commerce operating as trade between islands around that time was as follows; *kumara, red feathers, taro, gourd, obsidian, animals, yams, pottery, coconuts, poultry and bananas.*

Worthy of note:
Red, being a rarity in the Pacific (including hair), held mystical powers sacred to the Tahitian god *'Oro,'* and was used as a type of currency; the red coloured parrot feathers were interwoven into ceremonial dress of high priests and chieftains.

The Manila Galleons:
The first Spanish vessel to sail the Pacific was commanded by none other than the Portuguese navigator Ferdinand Magellan (Fernando de Magallanes) 1480 -1521 AD. It was only later that the Spanish developed commercial shipping routes from Lima in Peru in South America to Manila in the Philippines; these ships had sailed within a host of islands

throughout the Pacific as discovered by the Spanish Pacific Fleet; the islands are as follows;

1521 Tuamotu islands, Marianas Islands, Cebu Island, Philippines, 1549. Galapagos, 1564 Guam, 1566 Marshall, 1567 Henderson, 1568 Soloman Islands. Marutea, Marquesas 1576. Easter (Rapa-nui, Pukapuka, Rarotonga, New Zealand and Tahiti 1606. (Note: some dates differ).

These vessels would have also carried the sweet potatoes *(kumara)* and certainly could use them as trade-off for fresh provisions where applicable. The galleons were used for silk and porcelain trade from mainland China, also spices that had been delivered by Arabs to the Philippines; these at the time were in great demand in America and Europe. 48.

Celtic Origins?
It's also interesting to note when the Polynesian Marquesas and the Caroline Island of *'Rakahanga'* in the Cook Group were discovered, the Spanish navigator 'Quiros' in 1595 mentioned that the natives were 'very white and very agreeable in appearance, tall, strong, large limbed, and so well made that they surpassed us, one lad as beautiful with golden hair as to see a painted angel'. Mendana also wrote that the Marquesas people were slim, graceful, of a light honey colour complexion, the woman and children as fair as Europeans.'
By the time Cook arrived almost two hundred years later on his second voyage, he mentioned that the natives were finely shaped with regular features that surpassed all other nations. 9, 48.

Spanish navigation:
To sail a galleon at four to six knots with the prevailing winds and currents towards the Philippines from Lima, one would sail west at approximately 15 degrees latitude. They couldn't use longitude

correctly as it hadn't been worked out at that stage. The favored route took in *Rapa Nui* (Easter Island), *Marquesas, Samoa*, then deviated down to *Vanuatu* and then up again to the *Santa Cruz, Santa Isabel Islands* in the Solomons, deviating again towards and around *Guadalcanal, New Guinea,* then passed through the *Torres Strait* above Cape York, Australia before sailing north of the eastern side of *Borneo* and finally to *Manila* in the Philippines.

On their return voyages the Spanish sailors had tried to sail back directly to Lima from Manila against the prevailing winds and tides without much success and finally abandoned the idea altogether, as many ships were lost or crews perished either from starvation or scurvy, usually both. It was only by chance that one of their ships in 1565, the *San Lucus* under the command of Captain Urdaneta, had been blown north by a tropical storm thus finding the westerly trades winds at 40 degrees, enabling them to sail easterly towards the coast of California, then upon arrival set another course south towards Acapulco and on to Lima. 9.

Madagascar:

There is written report of trading vessels visiting Madagascar being multi-hull outrigger canoes, some with double *amas* on either side, *tri-hull* or a single float attached to the main hull *proa* that used the method of *shunting,* a sailing technique where the mast is moved manually. The dialect spoken by the crew was said to be Polynesian, this is also has to be a myth, *why?*

Madagascar is a large island situated in the western sector of the Indian Ocean close to the African East Coast; their culture at the time being more intelligent than the former, they would have been a major threat to the Pacific people as slavery was and is still widespread with privateers and pirates looking for easy prey. Any Polynesian crew in such waters would have been fair game. It would seem more logical that past scholars found the Polynesian dialect was similar to Tamil-Indian, thus presumed the Polynesians had at some stage sailed there. Also the fact that out-rigger multi-hull sailing vessels were and are still to be found in abundance around the Indian Ocean regions, the forerunner of Polynesian sailing outriggers had come from the Indian Ocean folk; thus adopted by the people of the Pacific. 20, 45, 48.

Canoe voyages to Peru?
From a seaman's point of view the *Waka* couldn't have sailed directly to South America from any South Pacific Island below the Equator as this feat alone would be almost beyond human endurance, *why?*

A replica double hulled 60ft *Waka* (not made of today's modern materials) with a full load had recorded an average speed between six and eight knots, weighing twenty-five tons, with a crew of fifty having sweeps/rudders measuring twenty-one feet in length, making over 190-200 nm in 24hr period achievable only in ideal conditions. Nevertheless, to sail east over such vast distances against the Humboldt Current (two and half knots with a flow to the west being approximately thirty-sixty nautical miles per 24 hour day) having prevailing head winds of various strengths, starting out say, from Henderson near Pitcairn Island sailing direct to Lima, a distance of 2-3000 nautical miles, to me seems extremely doubtful.

One can rule out paddle power as a twenty five ton canoe would need fresh crews with stamina/energy on a daily basis - certainly not possible. Even if sailing in a straight line from Henderson Island with favourable winds from astern it would take months to reach Peru as the combined headwinds and tidal flow would bring on tremendous seas. Furthermore, at that latitude there are calms that will delay sailing vessels for weeks on end and the Humboldt Current is also famous for having ice cold, damp, foggy conditions, meaning longer uncomfortable periods at sea.

A voyaging *Vaka*, depending on the type of rigging, would need to tack (*zigzag*) at 75 degrees angle into the wind, whereas a modern sailboat can tack at 45 degrees or less, thus making the canoe voyage at least three times the distance. Being realistic, to sail to Lima, the route taken would have been at a different angle of degree using the combined wind and tide shifts as an advantage by sailing further southeast from *Henderson* towards either *Easter, Juan Ferndez* or perhaps *San Felix Islands,* then once loaded with fresh provisions, continued onwards towards Peru allowing for a favourable sea state and wind conditions.

However, to sail above the Equator from the Marquesas to Peru would only be possible using the northeast or the northwesterly seasonal trade winds. The same would apply when sailing to Hawaii from the Marquesas group after the northern cyclone season November – May, a voyage made possible using the islands in between such as *Christmas, Kirimati, Palmyra* and *Johnston* as refreshment stopovers.

Nevertheless, a voyage in the opposite direction to New Zealand from the *Marquesas* or the *Cook Island Group,* the Polynesian native would have island hopped *(puddle jumping)* using the prevailing easterly and southeasterly trades using the Humboldt Current for a swift passage, leaving April - November after the southern cyclone season, and calling at various atolls and islands along the way taking in the *Cooks, Tonga, Samoa, Wallis/Futuna, Fiji, Kermadec* and the *Three Kings*, the latter an island situated above North Cape within visual distance from Northland, *Aotearoa,* New Zealand. 9, 20, 28, 29, 42, 48.

Easter Island (Rapa Nui): (27 .05 degrees south/109 .22 degrees west). *View Google Map.*

This whole island is only about one hundred and seventeen square km, has three ancient extinct volcanoes, and is almost inaccessible by boat due to high cliffs surrounding it. At the time of discovery by the Dutch Admiral Jacob Roggeveen in, c.1722, he found the island of *Rapa-nui* to be barren without trees, having poor soil and looking from a distance to be a sandy island. However, when explored the ship's crew noticed that the whole island looked to be totally abandoned as there were no sentries posted to watch the coastline in case of enemy attack. Instead they found a race of natives who thought they were the only people on the planet, and were actually terrified at the sight of white Europeans. Prior to this time as word has it the native Polynesian Maori found the island in 400AD to be covered in forest and scrub, this had been gradually cleared making way for crops, and later due to over population, lack of food and water created in-fighting for control, forcing another mass migration, but according to modern science this is also a myth, *why*?

* The first people were stone masons - a highly specialized culture who cut, polished, and placed precisely shaped stones to make dwellings and set up pillars of stone in alignment for solstice seasonal observations.

* The second settlers, also stone masons, had no knowledge of the planetary system. They had erected stone walls, stone and scrub/sod type dwellings, and also obtained the art of cutting out giant size statues from solid rock, referring to the free-
standing long-eared *'Moai'* obelisk objects.

* The third inhabitants were not stone masons but primitive wood carvers, a destructive warring people who destroyed the previous working by toppling the obelisk Moai statues and destroying the

astronomical sites. They also constructed communal long houses like those found in the jungle of South America in the shape of a large canoe hull upside down with a side entrance near the centre - a communal building. Scholars believe that all the above are South American natives except for the latter to be of Polynesian stock who were not Maori so who were they?

On Cook's second voyage in *Resolution* in 1774 he found the Easter Island natives friendly and unarmed, bringing gifts of produce in canoes made from driftwood logs. Cook found the island to be treeless, having no animals; they did have domestic poultry, potatoes, taro and sugarcane, but he noted the food shortage. The drinking water from the extinct volcanoes craters he found too brackish to replenish his ship and mentioned that the stone idols were clearly not Polynesian. When questioned the Rapa-nui natives had no explanation of them, said the idols had always been there. 9, 48. *(Online).*

<u>The distance from Easter Island is as follows:</u>
1500 miles to Mangareva,
2000 miles to Pitcairn and Tahiti,
2300 miles to Chile in South America,
3800 miles to New Zealand.

<u>Why not Maori?</u>
The latter natives on Easter Island built elongated houses, they were primitive wood carvers, a destructive, small, timid miserable people, and they even had language difficulties – they didn't understand what was said when speaking to *'Otiti,'* Cook's Tahitian interpreter using the Polynesian tongue. Furthermore, they used double head axes, double blade canoe paddles, worshipped a god called *'Mekemeke'* and didn't worship Polynesian deities such as *Tane, Maui, Tiki, Tangaroa, Tu,* or *Rongo,* they cremated their dead (completely foreign to Polynesia), and

even developed script a written language carved on wood similar to the Cuna Indians from the Sanblas Islands in the Atlantic. Scholars now believe the latter had arrived from the west as Polynesians whilst the previous two cultures came from the east, being of South American decent. Nevertheless, when found by Europeans the natives' health problems were many - that may have been a result of poor hygiene and inbreeding. More importantly, at the time of discovery the Dutch Admiral Jacob Roggeveen noted that the *Rapa Nuians* had *pineapples, gourd, banana, sugarcane, chickens, kumara, tobacco,* even having a *written language (word)* and use of the *bow*. It is also interesting to know that the bow could be found in the 'Kingdom of Tonga' a Melanesian culture; it had also been used in the *Marquesas* group and *Tahiti;* the latter two being *Polynesian* Islands. Moreover, scholars found that *Rapa Nuians* had the knowledge of the *bow, sling, throwing darts (spears);* the latter recent finds were found in old lava tunnels as if the people had been hiding from an enemy within them. 42, 45, 48. (Online).

The mystery deepens:
I was in the poultry business for 25 years; I know this breed of chicken's native country is Asia, not the Americas. As these birds are of tropical origin they are not the usual domestic breed of fowl as found in European countries; it would have more likely been introduced to Easter Island by Chinese whilst sailing their massive teak ocean-going 200ft sailing ships when visiting the Pacific in 1421.
Nevertheless, tobacco was in use amongst the natives of Central America when found by Columbus in 1492, suggesting the *Rapa Nui'ans* must have contacts with the mainland as they in addition had *tobacco,* an Asian breed of *chicken,* the art of *pottery,* plus written *word,* the *sling and bow.* 6.

Question
Here we have a totally different type of weaponry - the *sling* and *bow* as found throughout the Pacific. Then especially *tobacco* being an addictive-type drug as recorded by European explorers. The bow however had been used throughout Melanesia and Polynesia (but for some reason not taken up by Maori as it would have been ideal for hunting birds and other game). The point I want to draw the reader's attention to is that the native Maori couldn't have ventured as far as *Rapa Nui;* if they had there would have been evidence of *tobacco,* the craft of *pottery,* written *word*, use of the *bow* and the knowledge of *stone masonry* within their culture. 6, 9, 20, 21, 27, 42, 44, 46, 52.

Worthy of note
In 1970 some DNA taken from Easter Islanders possessed A29 and B12 heliotype genes, characteristic of the European Caucasoid as the *Rapa Nui'an* natives were a light coloured people more so than the Polynesian, perhaps a result of the past European sailors having relations with the island women folk.

Sling Shot as Weaponry:
Captain Abel Janzoon Tasman's logbook mentions that upon his arrival in New Zealand 1642 they anchored their two ships *Zeehaen* and the *Heemerkirk* in what is known today as 'Golden Bay' near the City of Nelson in the northern sector of South Island; it was here that they were greeted by a number of warring Maori who came out from shore in canoes. As the custom for Maori, they gave out a challenge *'Haka'* (war dance) and also sounded the conch shell which was mistaken by Tasman as a type of greeting. He then replied using bugles. By then it was late evening and the natives returned and prepared for warring ashore whilst the Tasman's crew, unaware of what they had started, went about their normal duties. Early next morning the natives returned in eleven canoes ready for action and once again the Maori gave their

challenging 'Haka' and sounded the conch shell - the latter a signal for the use of slingshot. Tasman's crew were startled, some being seriously hurt, with the end result being that a 'cockboat' whilst shuttling to the other vessel was rammed by a *waka* with four members of the crew killed and eaten. *(Melanesian custom # five).*

The slingshot had also been used as mentioned by Cook when visiting the 'Bay of Plenty' New Zealand 1769 where a double canoe approached *Endeavour* and pelted the ships with stones, damaging her aft windows 22, 48.

Pre - Maori:
There were five distinct groups of cultures already in Aotearoa by the time of the arrival of Maori so to lessen the confusion between the five cultures I've allowed the following; 4, 7, 9, 20.

(1) The *'Moriori/Maru-iwi/Nga-iwi'* of *Melanesian* decent.
(2) The *'Waitaha'* the Children of *Maui*.
(3) The *'Patu-pai-arehe'* of Celtic decent.
(4) The *'Turehu'* the People of Heaven.
(5) The *Uru-kehu* the Children of Kiwa.

Chapter Three:

A dishonest act, Who really discovered New Zealand, Buried alive, Other small folk, The Australian Barrinean Pigmy, Pre-Maori historical sites, Secretive digs, Lake Taupo volcanic eruption 186AD, Further evidence, Headstone, Factual findings 1860, Patupaiarehe inhabitants, Modern findings 2009.

<u>A dishonest act:</u>
In most countries all historical written records and artifacts that go back in time have been carefully restored, numbered accordingly, and proudly displayed in museums as an educational tool, a fact finding service for all age groups. However, in New Zealand for some reason our politicians carried out the opposite as if trying to cover up all pre-Maori history. It's an absolute disgrace to think that pre-Maori records and artifacts about the early New Zealand settlers have been gradually removed from our national museums, libraries and schools starting with Auckland 1998 and as far south to the Otago Museum Dunedin in the South Island, why? 4, 33.

<u>Who really discovered New Zealand?</u>
The *Waitaha* also known as *Patu-pai-arehe, Turehu* or *Kiritea* are believed to be the true indigenous people of New Zealand going back 5000 years or more, with one tribe of *Patu-pai-arehe* being decimated by the warlike Maori who invaded the islands 7-600 BP *'Landed Aliens' (Tautangata).* Today some Maori hold the view that the *Patu-pai-arehe* folk are just a myth whilst others believe that they are the real ancestors. Perhaps a further DNA testing should be carried out to set

this record straight? To settle an argument once and for all about the earlier folk I've included the following article; *BP before present.*

'Northern Advocate Newspaper, Wednesday 21st, December, 2005.'
A new cache of *'Turehu'* (a subgroup of the *Patu-paiarehe*) bones have been found in the Kaipara District. The skeletons are being studied by Noel Hilliam, former Curator of the Dargaville Maritime Museum and his team of researchers. There were at least three distinct physical types of *Patu-paiarehe* living in New Zealand, ranging from the very tall people (around 7 to 8 feet in height 2.4 metres) to people of normal stature down to the very small white pygmy people with golden-white hair and large blue eyes. Being small in stature the *'Turehu'* were a particularly attractive childlike people with very fine features, they are referred to as *'Te Whanau O Rangi'* (the people of heaven) in Maori oral tradition. These small people once populated countries like Ireland and traditions concerning their occupation of the Pacific range from Tahiti, New Caledonia to New Zealand.

Above; one of many photos taken by Noel Hilliam of the very small stature *Turehu* people that he and a group of experts are secretly studying. Noel's attempts to undertake proper scientific investigation on behalf of the New Zealand public are being thwarted and blockaded by the PC establishment. He is also disallowed access to forensic testing facilities within New Zealand. As with all other skeletal finds these remains would be destroyed if the authorities could gain access to them. *Article & photo provided by Noel Hilliam. (Online).*

Buried alive?
To add to this confusion there is more evidence that has been photographed and records taken of corpses, once thought to be children until a dentist explained that their skulls showed full sets of adult teeth, a forest dwelling *nocturnal people,* our very own New Zealand *Turehu* Pigmy being only four and a half feet tall. The remains were bound with flax fiber before death, they were buried alive. *(Melanesian custom # six).*

Worthy of note:
Whilst we were in Vanuatu a group of archeologists and anthropologists uncovered an ancient burial mound southwest of the township of Vila with finds of human remains each bound with fibre cordage. These gruesome finds had once been rituals that took place upon a death of a chieftain and as the custom his extended family including loyal followers been given 'Kava' then once intoxicated all were bound and buried alive. To celebrate their new chief, fellow members of the remaining tribe danced on top of the burial site thus packing it down making sure nobody remained alive.

Other small folk:
It is also interesting to note that similar finding of skeletal remains of '*Homo Floresiensis*', small, one metre high forest dwellers (also nocturnal), had been found in Liang Bua Cave on 'Flores' *(Island of flowers)* in Java. Also the Hawaiians tell of a race of small people that they called **Menehune** when the present Hawaiians landed. The same applies in the Society Islands (*Tahiti*) where they were called the **Manahune** folk. Again, this time in Samoa, little folk, all forest dwellers,

existed on the islands before the arrival of the descendants of *Tangaloa,* who mentioned that these dwarf people were produced from worms grown from rotting vines. Even on the island of *Moorea,* another of the Tahitian group, an exceptional finds of *fairy folk with golden hair* had been discovered. In the Kingdom of Tonga there was an inferior social caste of little folk, and in Australia there was a small forest-dwelling people called the **Barrineans** that were only four to five foot in stature. Furthermore, there is another report of dwarf size folk, the **Dropa Tribe**, in *Sichuan Province* in China - unbelievably small at 2 to 4 foot in height. Even today one can still find pygmies in the highlands forests of Africa and on 'Espiritu Santo', an island in the Vanuatu group.

Throughout the world pygmies were recorded in Ireland, South America, Thailand, Africa, Java, Malaysia, PNG, Indonesia, Philippines, Brazil, SE Asia, China, Micronesia, Melanesia, Australia, Hawaii, Samoa, Tonga, Tahiti and New Zealand. In all the above countries there is no mention of small people having fair skin and multi-coloured hair except for *Ireland, America, Tahiti, Caroline Island, Marquises* and *New Zealand.* 3, 16, 31, 33, 46. *(Online).*

The Australian Barrinean Pygmy:
I wanted to bring the reader's attention to our nearest neighbour because of some interesting facts that in one or two cases closely relate to the Polynesian Maori. According to scholars Australia has been peopled for over 60,000 years, perhaps longer, by the Aboriginal native. It is also interesting to note the *Ngadjon* small folk have only recently been brought to the attention of the media. At the time of discovery there were only twelve tribes of approximately seven hundred people living in isolated groups around Lake Barrine in the Atherton Tablelands, believed to have arrived in Queensland 40,000 years ago.

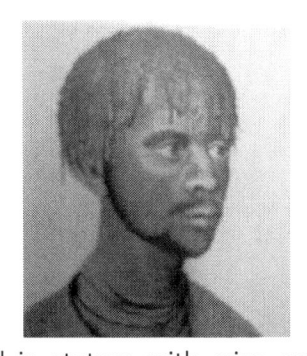

These folk were small in stature with crisp curly hair, similar to the people of Africa, who are not related to mainland Aborigine, Tasmanians, Melanesians, nor the Polynesians, so where did they actually come from? According to *Ngadjon* folklore they came from the south but although they have similar features and culture to Tasmanian natives, their DNA samples suggest otherwise. It's also interesting to note that they built domed huts lasting several years, made *tapa* cloth bark blankets, learnt to live in accordance with nature and never against it, used fire sticks, adapted to rain forest environmental conditions successfully, carried babies in baskets made of cane hanging from mothers' backs attached to bands around their foreheads somewhat like the African native, and made grass/flax-type baskets like their Tasmanian and New Zealand cousins. The *Barrine* small folk skilfully trapped animals, birds and fish, and were known to be peaceful, definitely not cannibalistic. Like the *Waitaha*, they held nocturnal ceremonies and used message sticks like the North American Indian, valued all life, killed only when hungry, didn't damage trees or scrub, and were not a destructive people – they respected the land. It was even a sin to kill an animal then throw it away; they caught only enough for the day and never more than needed, having no waste. Like the New Zealand native, they left no one without relatives. Also worth remembering: the oldest male had the right to supervise affairs in each community, and having to share things is an important part of their culture, not to be greedy. Moreover, the weapons, made from fire-hardened wood, were used were only for defence purposes, such as spears, cross shaped boomerangs, large flat broadswords with decorated wooden shields *(Online)*.

Tasmanian & Mainland Aborigines Differ:

Triganini was the last of her line as a Tasmanian aborigine originally from Bruny Island, situated southeast of Hobart. A complete skeleton of Triganini was on show in the Hobart Museum where we as a family personally saw her in 1974. After that DNA samples were taken before her removal, and her ashes were scattered over the sea off Bruni Island. Whilst in 'Tassie', as the locals call their island state, I found that the only way for me to get the true feeling of this 'Apple Isle' was to study their history, which I found rather disturbing. I had been informed that the Native Tasmanians were treated as pests simply because they were nomadic hunters who made the grave mistake of slaughtering one or two farm animals for food. This I found later wasn't the true reason they were slaughtered, but in those days the settlers didn't mess around and eventually killed off the Taswegians by placing a bounty on their heads.

The Tasmanian natives were extremely hardy people, totally different from the mainland aborigine, with a different culture, facial features, language, fire sticks, (these were always found in their possession, punishable by death if extinguished), mud plastered hair to attract warmth, wrap around clothing made from animal hides, huts made of tree branches or logs stacked in such a way that it took a form of a tepee without animal hides; had the bow and darts for weapons, but lacked the *boomerang* and *woomera* (a leverage stick attached to end of spears as used by their mainland cousins). If anything, these people actually resembled the culture of Tierra del Fuego *'Ona'* Indians in southern Chile. *(View; Ona Indians online).*

Pre - Maori historical sites:
It has been recorded that old pre-Maori historical sites have been deliberately destroyed using bulldozers to cover burial cave sites, flattening stone walls and ancient buildings. *Why?*

Unbelievably, there was once a forest city in Northland of 2000 stone 'domed hemispherical' structures; these dwellings were made from stone slabs without mortar that had a keystone fitted in the centre of the domed roof, with entrances just large enough for a small adult to pass through. In all a truly amazing piece of engineering. These small enclosures were spaced over 200ha and were believed to be thousands of years old. There were even drainage systems with massive earthworks, and ancient channels throughout the region where swamp lands had been cleared providing large sections of arable land for cropping/vegetable production, so who were these people? Maori technical knowledge wasn't advanced enough to build dwellings of stone; they at the time of European exploration were recognized as savages, a fierce, treacherous people who devoured their own, a primitive stone-age cannibalistic race. Nevertheless, the ruins of the same type of stone domed dwellings, now flattened, can still be seen in and around the Auckland district, such as the *Tapapakanga Park* near 'Orere Point' south east of the city and five other sites around Northland. These factual sites have been carbon dated and are believed to be approximately 5000 years old. The same applies to a site in the

Waipoua Forest in Northland, a Department of Conservation public property now made *'Tapu/Taboo'* (Forbidden/Sacred) by the local *iwi*, Te Roroa hapu, (sub tribe), known as the Waipoua Archaeological Advisory Committee. *Why?* 4, 13.

Secretive Digs:

In the late 1980s our New Zealand Government had archaeological assessment made of the above Northland site at considerable expense to the tax payer ($650,000 NZD) and as results of these digs the site had an embargo placed on it. Fourteen pages of carbon dating were removed from the fact finding report which was to be locked away in the archives for 75 years and not to become accessible until the year 2063, dated 7th September 1988. The carbon dating documents have never been released to the general public, only to a selected few, and are now considered a threat to National Security. Wanting to further our research into these digs we sent an email letter to the National Archives of New Zealand at the Auckland Regional Office requesting a copy of the above; the Archives replied with the following statement: 4, 13.

'There is no access restrictions in place for public viewing or to the records referred to in this list.'

Furthermore, we manage to obtain from the Archives through Hon John Carter, Northland MP, two copies;
(A) hand written copies of the manuscript, (B) typed photocopies of the all the above finds, with references dating as far back as early to 1951, including finds of artifacts with reference numbers for each item, also attached reference to the radiocarbon dating; Waipoua Forest 1983. (BBEE A1234/1c).
But there was no evidence available to the public from the actual radiocarbon dated report.

The Waipoua Forest finds are as follows; pits, stone structures, stone walls, hangi pits, stone terraces, water channels, mega heap, trenches, adze drawings, stone artifacts, and drawings. Another disturbing find mentions a file with a statement giving *'Te Kopae Authorities'* permission to damage, modify and destroy archaeological sites. *Why?*

Worthy of note:
The above embargo is only one out of 105 cases, mostly concerning burial sites, now classified as so-called 'Sensitive Files.' For those who want to follow through with the above, I suggest contacting the Archives references: (BAIHA617) and copies (A617). *Auckland@archives.govt.nz*

Since the early 1970s there has been a deliberate attempt to rewrite history to promote the view that Maori are the true indigenous people, also such things as rampant cannibalism or practices of slavery among Maori are being combed out of history books and at times substituted with mystical and euphoric fairy-tale themes that downplay violence and promote an idyllic quality of existence. *Why?*

Lake Taupo volcanic eruption 186 AD:
About twenty-odd years ago there was a massive landslide on the shores of Lake Taupo. This was due to a storm creating havoc, with slips wearing away pumice and topsoil from the 186 AD massive Taupo volcanic explosion, believed to be ten times larger than the Krakatoa eruption, which was heard as far away as England. An old lava tunnel was exposed, and inside, scholars found skeletons of humanoids that may have died as a result of the Taupo explosion. This was at a time when no one was meant to be living in New Zealand. If this holds true, who were these ancient people and what happened to the skeletal remains? Were there any radio carbon tests or DNA taken, or did

someone authorize to have these skeletal remains removed and deliberately destroyed? 17. *(Online)*.

Further evidence:
In 1940 and once again in 1975 there were two separate finds of skeletal remains near Wairoa township on the East Coast that had their legs crossed and arms folded against their chests, looking out to sea. It is believed they were buried that way to draw in pilot whales to shore; this is not a Maori custom, it is believed to be *Moriori*. 18, 23.

Headstone:
Further proof of the actual existence of the *Waitaha* people can be found in the city of Dunedin, where a headstone in the 'Colac Bay Cemetery' has an inscription of the deceased as a leading chieftain of the '*Waitaha, Ngati-mamoe* and the *Ngati-ahu Tribes.*' 26.

Factual findings:
Up to 1869 the Northland farmers found skeletons everywhere, in the bush, scrub, even caves and tunnels, as if an ethnic cleansing had taken place, as it looked as though the unfortunates were caught unaware and herded together and then systematically executed. The Colonial police/troopers, farmers and government officials approached the local *Iwi* (Tribes) near *Te kopuru* with the Governor General of New Zealand, then Sir George Ferguson Bowen G.C.M.G., in attendance. At the *Hui* meeting were a gathering of *kaumatua, Tohungas* and *Rangitira* (elders and chieftains) who heard Bowen ask to which tribe did these skeletal remains belong, and what could be done? The chieftain's response; *"Do what you wish, for these are not our people."* A work party was then organized using horse drawn wagons which were loaded with the skeletal remains, then they were taken to Dargaville, placed in barges, and shipped to Onehunga near Auckland City where they were ground

by windmill into bone meal. After three years the skull count came to a total of 60,000 bodies. *NZ Gazette, National Archives 1869.*

The old Mt Eden windmill, situated in the Auckland suburb of Onehunga, was first built by William Mason in 1843 for grinding grain. When a more efficient water powered mill was created, this windmill passed into the ownership of others including Mr. Robert Robertson, and in the 1860s was used to grind up the skeletal remains of countless generations of *Patu-paiarehe* into fertilizer. Many thousands of skeletons were removed from the Auckland burial caves for this purpose and sold to the mill. Maori at the time had no concerns about the fate of the remains of the *Tangata whenua* (first people).

There is a New Zealand stamp that was designed and put together by a former friend of my wife Sylvia, the late Manu Smith from Waiheke Island, which was his attempt to portray the *Patu-paiarehe* people that lived in New Zealand for hundreds of years before the coming of Maori. It seems every iwi (tribe) has legends about these people and the learned elders can still point out the high country locations where the *Patu-paiarehe* lived. In fact all aspects of Polynesian Maori culture, such as the flax fibre fishing nets, greenstone carving etc, were derived from these people as either taught or gained through the spoils of war and conquest. Maori described these ancient *'stone builders'* as *Kiri-puwhero* and *Uru-kehu,* which means people who had reddish or blond tinged hair and a light complexion. The *Patu-paiarehe* were also known as fairy folk, a race of fair skinned people, with blue or green eyes, having childlike features, many with a wealth of red or fair hair. Some lived in the Rotorua district and in *Tuhoe* land, *'Children of the mist'* in the Urewera country around Lake Waikaremoana, (our family stomping grounds). This lake and another smaller Waikare-iti are situated between the inland township of Murupara and Wairoa on the East Coast. Here the *Patu- paiarehe* stayed and hid in the bush, only coming out at night while Maori occupied the lakeside. Unfortunately the *Patu-pai-arehe* women, once captured, were kept as slaves whilst adult males were slaughtered and eaten. This was known by Maori as 'Walking the Land' - a conquest for land rights ownership? One must remember that cannibalism was rife in Melanesia but rare in Polynesia. 13, 16, 18, 33, 48. *(BP Before present).*

Patupaiarehe inhabitants:
The following was written by Hoani Nahe, an *Ngati Maru* (Hauraki) Maori elder of the late century. He quotes as follows;

'When the migration arrived here they found people living in the land, **Ngati Kura, Ngati Korakorako** *and* **Ngati Turehu***, all sub-tribes of a people called* **Patu-pai-arehe***. The chiefs of this people were named Tahurangi, Whanawhana, Nukupori, Tuku, Ripiroaitu, Tapu-te-uru and Te Rangipouri. The dwelling places of these people were on the sharp peaks of the high mountains – those in the district of the Hauraki (Thames) are Moehau Mountain (Cape Colville), Motutere (Castle Hill, Coromandel), Maumaupaki, Whakairi, Te Koronga, Horehore, Whakaperu, Te Aroha-a-uta, Te Aroha-a-tai, and lastly Pirongia, at Waikato. The pa and houses of these people are not visible, nor actually*

*seen by mortal (Tangata Maori) eyes – that is, their actual forms. But sometimes these people are met with by the Maori people in the forest, and are heard conversing and calling out, as they pass along, but at the same time they never meet face to face, or so that they mutually see one another, but the voices are heard in conversation or shouting, but the people are never actually seen. On some occasions also during the night, they are heard paddling their canoes. At such times are heard these questions: 'What is it? Who are the people who were never heard urging forward their canoes on the sea during the night or who were heard conversing and shouting in the forest? They were not Tangata Maori; they were the **Atua, Patupaiarehe, Turehu**, or the **Korakorako**.' End Quote. 25, 33. (Online).*

<u>Modern findings 2009:</u>
The 'Ruamahunga River Skull' was subjected to a round of DNA and age tests that confirmed it to be from a European woman aged from 40 to 45 years old who was *'well and truly alive in New Zealand from about 1619 to 1689.'* That's before Abel Tasman discovered New Zealand in 1642 or the arrival of Captain James Cook in 1769. The DNA test was conducted by Dr Leon Huynen at Massey University. It had been discounted as unlikely to be a medical specimen because it was very old and found far from a city and miles out in the countryside, also there were no catalogue or code marks. *Wairarapa Times – Age 30th November 2009 (online).*

Chapter Four:

The International road show, Juan Fernandez, Taniwha dragon, Kiore, black rat, The Moa Hunters, Native dogs,(Kuri), Massive earthquake, Oldest record of man in New Zealand, Musket tribal wars, The three main reasons for the treaty.

<u>'The International Road Show'</u>
The National Museum had a display called the *'Vaka Moana Touring Global Exhibition',* an educational tool for all to see about the arrival of the Maori to New Zealand. Once we had seen and admired the displays and splendid amount of input given, we felt extremely proud of what had been achieved. There is also a large book of the same name that we found simply brilliant, and to us it was more appealing than the exhibition itself, giving detailed information about the arrival of the Maori, but we felt disappointed that the truth hadn't all been told as the *'Vaka Moana Touring Global Exhibition'* and its book tell that the Maori were the first people to settle New Zealand.

All our personal findings, plus positive input, combined with photographs and artifacts, suggest otherwise. It now seems that the road show is purely a propaganda machine designed to mislead the public and the world at large. **Why?** View; *aucklandmuseum.com*

<u>Question?</u>
Are our New Zealand politicians too embarrassed to let the truth be known? Or is it easier to let Maoridom take over and run its due course, knowing all along that the old Polynesian-Maori were not the first settlers in New Zealand? Or have they branded all Polynesians as Maori?

Moreover, our New Zealand Government members know beyond all reasonable doubt that the above finds are 'factual' – do they foolishly believe that all the concrete evidence presented before them about pre-Maori will be lost over a period of time? There are private collectors that we have met personally who won't let these facts be forgotten as they have kept copies of written material, photographic evidence and collections of artifacts, now hidden from government and other prying eyes. 52.

Juan Fernandez:
Juan Fernandez as one of the first Spanish explorers to New Zealand mentioned from his writings to the best of his judgment that New Zealand is a lovely fertile place.

'The inhabitants had been of fair complexioned people of the same height, good proportion and physical attributes, well dressed, of gentle and peaceful disposition. We were very well received and shown in every way they could express. The greatness of hospitality had been given, both with respect to the fruits and other products from the land, which appears in every way to have been rich and bountiful. The natives were very well dressed and wore white woven garments.'

Fernandez also noted that the way the Southern North Island natives carried their babies was different to Maori. It seems that Maori often referred to the same legendary *Turehu/Patu-pai-arehe* fairy-like folk; these as a people were not fairies but actually fairy-like having a fair complexion with soft flowing yellowish or red hair, they wore white garments quite different from Maori dress. Their children also had light, soft hair and weak eyes which could not stand sunlight; the same could be found with the Hawaiian *Menehune* small people. *(Online).*

Landed Aliens:

It has been recorded there have been other visitors to New Zealand before Maori that included Melanesians, Arabs, Portuguese, Celtic and Asians explorers, the latter with their own settlements around the Waikato coastal district near Raupuke, also another report of a construction site in the northern part of the South Island around the low swamp land near Blenheim, with another in Northland near Dargaville referring to ancient man-made canals. 4, 6, 21, 33, 48. *(Online).*

Taniwha/Dragon:

The mythical tale of an elusive reptile, often told by Maori to frighten children to stop them misbehaving or wandering off near rivers, lakes or bush, maybe true after all. During our research we came across an article that may be of interest for those within Maoridom and scholars alike as there is a mention of an eight *(pied)* foot lizard, or perhaps crocodile that attacked and devoured man, presumed to have lived in New Zealand before European exploration. Crocodiles are warm water creatures so perhaps this eight foot man-eater could have been a relative of the famous Komodo dragon, known as a Monitor lizard. Found on the islands around Indonesia, these mammals are massive, being up to ten feet in length, weighing approximately 300lbs/135 KG. Like our tuatara, they can live over 100 years. 46.

The kiore, black rat:
An international team of researchers from the National Academy of Sciences in the United States used their findings of radiocarbon dating of the bones of the Pacific rat or *kiore* to suggest that human colonization of New Zealand began around 730 BCE, or 2,741 BP. This theory I find interesting, knowing that it is possible to have small human colonies without rats, but I now feel it would have been more likely that the *kiore* rat had come from an earlier people and not with Maori as first believed. 6, 14, 19, 33, 44. *BCE before Common Era*
BP before present. (Online).

The Moa Hunters:
There were ten species of Moa, all flightless birds that once roamed the islands of New Zealand. The smallest was the *Bush Moa* weighing approximately 30kgs, and the largest was *Dinornis Maximus* with a height of approximately 9ft/3 metres weighing about 170kgs. The South Island *Waitaha* named it *Kuranui* whilst the *Ngati Porou* on the East Coast of the North Island knew it simply as *Moa*, (Chicken) but when questioned by Europeans it seems that Maori didn't know of its existence, until given the required information. Skeletal remains of these giant creatures had been found around fire pits and middens, along with the extinct eagle, swan, and crow, with others including seals, porpoises, whales, *rats*, birds, lizards, *dogs*, dolphin, and shellfish - with the majority of finds being in the South Island. Radiocarbon dates these bones at 1100 AD, that's before Maori arrived in 1350. Moreover, the 'Moa Hunters' used stone tools such as flaked obsidian/volcanic glass as stone knives, stone spearheads, stone adzes, and stone fish hooks, with some so highly polished as to be noted as outstanding features.

If the above holds true the first natives, the real *(Tanga Whenua)* had *dogs* and the *native rat* long before the arrival of Maori, indicating that the 'Moa Hunters' were a different race of people altogether.

Nevertheless, battle weapons such as the *patu* and *mere* were not of their culture; as mentioned the Moa Hunters were certainly not the Maori of the so called great migration, nor were they cannibalistic, but were believed to be a nation of peaceful people called the *Waitaha*. 2, 44.

'We were welcomed by Uru-kehu and Maoriori, we gave them the knowledge. From a distance we looked like Uru-kehu with our hazel eyes, pale skin and red, fair hair yet face to face we were so different. They came from the four winds some dark some white and lived as one. 'Uru-kehu' children of Kiwa, the golden ones, the short people with freckled skin, blue eyes and fair, red hair. Then there were the 'Kiritea' also small, fair skinned, long black hair and green eyes.'

The figures on the right of a woman have all five fingers believed to be a 'Waitaha' carving as Maori allow only three as seen on the Hei Tikis.

It's interesting to note that the name for one of the Maori weapons is 'patu' and that this was a term for the earlier *Patu-paiarehe*, *kiri-puwhero* and *Uru-kehu*, meaning 'the greenstone folk' the stone builders also called *Turehu*. 15, 32, 44.

'Since the beginning of time lived at the centre of the island, a people who were wise, happy and loved by the Gods.' http://www.waitaha.org/

Native dogs, (Kuri):
Cook said he found the natives' dogs to be the ugliest creatures he had ever seen, being small in size, fox-like short legged creatures, similar to those found in Tahiti. Both species were known for their ugly long faces. The natives killed their canine for food by clasping both hands around the nose and jaw until asphyxiated, then skinned and gutted them

before placing them in umus/hangis/earth ovens. Some scholars believed the Polynesian native dog had forward pointed ears and a curled tail somewhat like the Husky. 32, 33, 46.

Note the Austronesian/Polynesian language differences;
Kuri for Maori or *Uri* in Tahitian, *Kuli for Tongan* and the word *Curi* in Welsh, (*Celtic*) all mean dog.
Tapu for Maori is also *Kapu* in Hawaiian, *Itambu* in Melanesian all mean sacred.
Kai for Maori is also *Kau* in Melanesian, meaning food.

Massive Earthquake:
Archeologists and anthropologists noted the abundance of midden sites around river estuaries in the South Island left by earlier pre-Maori natives but noted the lack of the same along the eastern coastal regions of the North Island. What the scholars may have overlooked, or weren't aware of, was that in the mid 1700s there had been a massive quake that submerged approximately fifteen miles of land to the east. This subsidence started in the northern sector of East Cape and went down along the coast to the Cook Strait, creating landslides that took out wildlife and native settlements. Furthermore, in the back country of the Urewera district landslides blocked valleys, rivers and streams to form what is now Lake Waikaremoana, *(Sea of Rippling Waters)*. Today however, one can see a submerged forest of massive tree trunks standing upright just below the surface - a danger to boating trout fishermen.

Another casualty of this quake was the Waipaoa River, the head being near to the settlement of *Whatatutu* in the back reaches of *Turanganui* district (Poverty Bay) near the modern city of Gisborne. The Waipaoa River was well known to *iwi* (tribes) as being the best source of travel by canoes to transit to the far southern reaches of the North Island to obtain access to the South Island via Cook Strait. Currently, the great Waipaoa River is partly covered by sea but the evidence still remains as charted by the Government Survey Ship *HMS Lachlan* whom I personally observed back in either the late 1950 or early 60s off the mouth of the Waipaoa taking soundings and samples. Charts now show this river had once run her full length from the Gisborne district around 'Young Nick's Head,' (*derived from a headland first sighted by Captain Cook's cabin boy 9th October, 1769*), through the narrow neck of the Mahia Peninsula where Opoutama Village now stands, to continue along the shores of the Wairoa district to finally flow inland taking in Hawkes Bay, Waipawa, Waipukurau, Takapau Plains, Dannevirke, Woodville, Pahiatua, and Masterton to flow into what is now known as Lake Waiarapa (*Shimmering Waters*) before exiting into the Cook Strait. Today one will notice stones and pebbles on the shoreline along the coastal regions of Hawkes Bay, also a vast amount of river metal found on the flats around Hastings, Waipawa, Waipukurau, Dannevirke, Takapau, Pahiatua, and the Waiarapa districts, giving evidence of what was once the longest river in New Zealand. (Dates of Cooks visit differ as some scholars suggest 6th October). 2, 32.

<u>The oldest record of man in New Zealand:</u>
The first government dam to be constructed on the Waikato River near the centre of the North Island was '*Arapuni*'. Building began in 1924 and it was commissioned in 1929. The dam was built with a curve and rose from the floor bedrock to a height of 64 metres/192ft. However in 1925 workers found a cave with moa bones within, and further back came across a headless human skeleton in solid rock, at least one hundred feet below the surface. If this find holds true, it suggests that the human remains would have been there for thousands of years, meaning that we will never know when or how long New Zealand had been occupied. The headless skeleton recorded was male, approximately 6ft in length, thin boned and believed to be Melanesian. Surely this find would have

made international news with photographic evidence, perhaps samples of the above may have been placed in a museum somewhere? If not already disposed of by *Iwi,* I suggest that to have 'DNA' Radiocarbon samples taken would give us the identity of race and approximate age of these extremely ancient people. 2, 45, 46. *(Online).*

<u>Worthy of note:</u>
Headless bodies were always buried, never burned or eaten; also the burial of people whilst still alive is definitely not a Maori custom. *<u>(Melanesian custom # seven).</u>*

<u>Musket Tribal Wars:</u>
It all started around the early 1810-20s when *Hone Heke,* a nephew of *Hongi Hika,* attacked settlers and other tribes around the Northland region using a combination of weapons such as the *patu, mere, taiaha* and the *kotiate,* all close combat weapons. These were useless against musketry, and the same could be said for the palisade, against the cannon. Maori needs for replacement weapons were met by *Pakeha* Europeans and the damage was devastating as total communities were completely annihilated especially in the Coromandel, Taranaki, Waikato districts and other areas throughout New Zealand, thus leaving vast open country without *iwi.* Maori intertribal fighting lasted around twenty years at a huge cost of 60-70,000 lives. *

The vacant lands were then sold by the warring Maori to *Pakeha* (Europeans) who resold the property in smaller lots for profit, mainly to settlers who built their cottages and turned the scrub/forest into farmlands.

The sailors, whalers, sealers, privateers and escaped convicts around the Bay of Islands back in those days were a Godless lot that brought complete lawlessness, especially around *Kororareka*, the township of Russell, then known as *'The Hell Hole of the Pacific'.*

The whaling and ships of trade came from Russia, Holland, France, Germany, Spain, Portugal, Britain, and the Americas. Most had the weapons required and were eager to swap them for flax and human tattooed heads. Greed for weaponry created more victims, even to the extent of Maori using their own slaves, forcing them to have facial tattoos, in exchange for weapons. The more facial markings the better the prize, and God help the young warrior with such a rich tattoo. Maori had taken land by force from other *iwi* tribes then sold it for whatever they could get. Today some would call it a priceless/senseless exchange but one has to realize that in those days Maori did not have use for money or precious metals, nor did we have any banking system then. Nevertheless, the native New Zealander could get muskets, powder and ball, nails, fish hooks, pipes, cooking pots, cotton, spades, hoes, knives, spikes, shovels, blankets, tobacco, food, spirits, beer, clothing, even footwear, and to Maori this was an extremely good bargain. 2, 32, 36, 37, 54. * *In some publications the numbers differ. (Online).*

The three main reasons for the Treaty: (Tiriti O Waitangi).
(1) The Musket Wars created panic with settlers especially the Northern, Waikato, Taranaki and Coromandel *iwi*/tribes to such an extent that the crown (NZ Government) was forced to bring in colonial forces from India and Australia to control the warring parties, to protect the friendly Maori and their own settlers.

(2) About the same period there was international interest from the French who were looking at starting settlements within New Zealand thus putting pressure on the Colonial Government. This was the beginning of such a threat that finally led to the signing of the original *Treaty of Waitangi* (on the fourth and not the sixth of February in 1840 as mentioned in history books), so designed to protect all New Zealand citizens.

(3) The other reason for the *treaty* was that the colonial government wanted to have a census taken of all the native population, but to do this the *iwi* had to have their own fixed locations. One must remember that the native Maori of *Aotearoa* at the time were mostly nomads, each moving from one location to another in search of better cultivated land and fishing grounds, even to the extent that if a lesser party were found to have such fertile soil and plentiful seas they were often challenged, thus bringing victory in battle that offered bonuses; women, slaves, and the addition of human flesh. The bottom line is that we all had our share of rogues in the past over land issues on both sides, not just Pakeha. The Maori always lived in fear and died young.

Burns writes; *'it's a race of wandering men and the population in any given place frequently varies. Sometimes these are no more than three thousand people in the Bay of Islands but at other times there are twelve thousand.'* 2, 15, 33, 34, 36, 37, 38, 39, 45, 46, 54. *(Online).*

Worthy of note:
Researchers arguably state the original treaty agreement has once again been deliberately tampered with since 1975, *why?* 34, 37, 54. *(View; 'From Treaty to Conspiracy' online)*

Chapter Five:

Genealogy/Whakapapa, The Ancient of Days, Let my people go, Shepherd Kings, Christian Education in New Zealand, Aramaic/Semitic language, New update, hawk (Kahu), Who are the True Indigenous People of New Zealand?

Genealogy/Whakapapa:
The first Pacific ethnic peoples were *Javanese, Melanesians, Micronesians,* and *Lapita,* believed to have come from Asia, had journeyed throughout the vast Pacific Ocean in a fan type formation approximately 60,000 years ago to include *Australia, Papua New Guinea, Philippines, Java, New Caledonia, Solomon, Vanuatu, Fiji,* and *Tongan* Islands. Then around 1500 years ago a new culture arrived, moving eastwards also in a fan type direction this time to include *Marquesas 300, Samoa, Cook, Society, Tuamotu, Tahiti, Rapa Nui, Hawaii,* 500-700 CE then down to *New Zealand* and even as far south as the *Auckland Islands,* the latter being about 600 CE.
Today an elderly Maori *Kaumatua* can trace their *Whakapapa* (Genealogy) back to the beginning by rote even to the location of their villages in the islands before their ancestors left for New Zealand, but little is known how and where they as a Pacific people came from previously before departing from Asia into the Pacific. We still have so much to learn from the Polynesian-Maori as to their true identity. To date, 'DNA' samples suggest that they came from *Taiwan,* an island off eastern mainland China, an Asian descent. Another positive sample came from '*India*'. All are true as Maori customs, language and art form show this, but more interesting is that these travellers as a people had

arrived in Asia from somewhere else before they headed eastwards across the Pacific. 2, 27, 28, 29, 30, 33, 45, 48. CE. Common Era.

Worthy of note:
Science has proven through the male 'Y' chromosome a tag exists that can trace one's ancestry back to its beginning but only through the female lineage. It's also interesting to know that the Hebrew could also trace their ancestry through the female lineage, than the male. It's interesting to note that the Hebrew DNA lineage has been found within the South American Indians, perhaps the Hebrew- Morman migration from West Africa 589 BCE.

The Ancient of Days:
My personal research shows that there is a strong link that goes back 2-1000 years BCE that may have some bearing in regards to tribal conflict. *(BCE; Before Common Era).*
In my college years in the 1960s I was involved with the study of Egyptology, and discovered that some of the Egyptian customs and spoken word to me seemed similar to Maori. It was this that drove me further into my research. Take for instance the ancient *'Sun God'*, called *'Ra'*, also the tattooing of chins, *mokos* for women and the facial markings of warriors as a sign of rank, also the nose greeting *hongi,* all Maori, it's also the same for the ancient Egyptians - all have a pedigree that goes back in time to the Bedouin Arabs. It seems incredible to think that two different cultures over a massive time span and vast distance could have the same name for an ancient god and also the facial tattooing and nose greetings *(exchange of breath)* that even in these modern times can still be found within Maoridom.
With this information I researched further with a minimal amount of success until someone pointed out to me the following amazing book that consisted of sixty-six manuscripts put together as one. It involves all our history from the beginning put together by thirty-nine authors over

1500 years. Even ancient writings of *Semitic Cuneiform Text* back up the following information now presented below.

The oldest *'proven'* history book would have to be the *'Torah, Pentateuch' (Heb)* or the *'Old Testament'* the *Christian Bible*. Historians, who a couple of centuries ago had no other source of information than a scattering of informational facts supplied by the Bible, found details of ancient cities; the precise locations, measurements of fortified walls, number of rooms, even where lay the treasured materials etc. Take for instance the great ancient cities of Nineveh and Babylon, the latter with its fortified walls so large and wide that chariot races were often held. These cities and others couldn't be located until researchers had gone through the ancient manuscripts. Only a handful of academics now admit that they had an enormous amount of material at their disposal and gratefully appreciate the input given from the *Tanakh (Heb) or The Old Testament*. 5, 8. *(Online)*.

<u>Let My People Go:</u>
Please bear with me on this one as there is evidence that could relate to Maoridom involving the people of *'Goshen'* as it was then called, now modern day Egypt. Both books *Tanakh (Heb)* and the *Christian Bible* tell us that the 'Hebrew' people were released from captivity in Egypt and led to the Promised Land guided by the God of Abraham, Isaac and Jacob using a type of mentor; *Exodus, Sh'mot (Heb.) chapters 1: verse 6*.

'Now there rose a <u>new King</u>/Pharaoh over Egypt. He knew nothing about Joseph, Yosef (Heb.) but said to his people, "Look, the descendants of Isra'el have become a people too numerous and powerful for us." So they put task masters over them to oppress them with forced labour.'

The Hebrew people were held over in slavery for a period of 400 years until a guy named Moses entered the scene. If possible make sure you read this to give an insight to the following especially about the plagues. After the Exodus, Egypt at that time was bankrupt; they had given the Hebrew people all the silver and gold - one of the main reasons why Pharaoh wanted to recapture them. *Sh'mot, (Heb.) Exodus 3: 21 – 23 & 10: 7.*

'And I will give this people favour in the sight of the Egyptians; and when you go, you shall not go empty, but each woman shall ask her neighbour and of her who sojourns in her house, jewelry of silver and of gold, and of clothing, and you shall put them on your sons and daughters; thus you shall despoil the Egyptians.'

And again; *Tehillim' (Heb) or 'Psalm' 105: 37 – 39.*

'Then he led his people out, laden with silver and gold; among his tribes not one stumbled, Egypt was happy to have them leave, because fear of Israel had seized them.'

As mentioned in the scriptures a disastrous event took place with Pharaoh's army being supernaturally annihilated. Egypt at that time was without an army/police force to defend its own people and as always in history this led to intertribal fighting between the 'Upper and Lower Nile' for control with the loser from the delta area having to move on.

The *Hykos* were a race of Asiatic people that ruled Egypt for nearly 150 years and came from ancient Mesopotamia, known then as *'The Crescent Belt'*, now modern Syria, Iraq and Iran, (14 – 16th Dynasty, 1648 - 1548 BCE.) They moved out and traveled in a north-easterly direction towards Pakistan, India, Bangladesh, Burma (now called

Myanmar) and lastly to Asia. Could it be that over the centuries these *Hykos* folk as they journeyed mixed, developed skills, adopted/copied customs of different cultures as they did in ancient Egypt? Being forced to leave; did they end up in Austroasia, then after a period of time find ways to cross the vast Pacific? We certainly think it was possible, as the *'Journey of Man'* talks about the great migration of people from Africa who traveled through the above mentioned countries. *(Torah, Pentateuch & King James Bible). 30, 31, 43, 53. BCE; Before Common Era.*

The Shepherd Kings:
The *Hykos* (Asian nomads) ruled Egypt during the Second Intermediate period of Egypt's ancient history, 1640-1550 BCE. They were driven out of the land by the last ruler of the 17th Dynasty, the earliest ruler of *'Egypt's New Kingdom'* as it was called this time, a real Egyptian pharaoh called Ahmose. *Dates differ as some scholars believe 1720-1560 BCE.*

The *Hykos* never ruled all of Egypt as the Upper and Lower Nile to the south was checked by border guards. The same applied for the borders northeast of Egypt being the *Shur Desert* of ancient *Kena'an* (Heb) Israel. In fact, something happened around the time of the exodus, for at Tell el- Dab'a (*Hykos settlement*) there was a find of mass graves with little attention to detail at the burial sites that could have been the result of a massive plague or disaster; moreover, no corpses or weapons of the slain *Hykos* Egyptian army have ever been found. When the *Hykos* were eventually driven out of Egypt, all traces of their occupation were removed. See *Sh'mot (Heb), Exodus chapter 7 – 14.*

The Hykos were a Semitic warlike people who introduced the composite bone bow and the chariot to Egypt and then moved down upon ancient *Kena'an* (Heb) Israel and through into Egypt slaughtering all before them. They adopted the ways of the Egyptians, making their capital in

Memphis. The chariot consisted of a platform that was balanced on two wheels, controlled by two or three warriors, one to guide the team of horses, the others covered and defending with poison tip spears, sword and bow. Their method of warfare was to make sure their foe were maimed or disabled, leaving their foot troops and their large trained dogs (believed to be greyhounds or mastiffs) to finish off the unfortunate victims. The Egyptians' opponents, like other invading armies around that time, would have been in large numbers as the norm was approximately; 62,000 infantry-men, 1,900 horsemen, 3,900 chariots and 1000 camels/donkeys, bronze weaponry and shields etc. In modern times this method of fighting would be like having an army of armored tanks and personnel-carriers bearing down upon you, whilst not having the same weaponry - a frightening situation to be in.

The earlier chariots mentioned in the scriptures were four-wheeled wagons, these were used to transport freight. *B'resheet, (Heb), Genesis 50: 8.*

What ever happened to honesty and integrity?
Sadly Christian Education has been removed from public schools, why? In the last census it was found that Christianity is in decline as it is a struggle to teach Biblical Scripture these days. The absence of firm principles or higher standards as guidelines for youth spells disaster for our society. Quotations from scripture will usually fall on deaf ears. The crux of solving today's problems in a modern society is to find an alternative prevention against crime.

Indo-Aryans:
Academics mention a particular race that moved directly towards India during the second Millennium BCE as a relocation of Indo-Aryans that passed down the eastern side of the Caspian Sea near the modern Iranian city of Tehran (ancient Persia), then separated into three groups,

the *'Mitannians'* and *'Kassites'* who moved towards the western sector of Iraq, whilst the others moved towards India. Such a movement of a large number of people would attract smaller alien groups of families joining the travellers with safety in mind, in so doing they naturally became part of a larger family of mixed cultures. It is also interesting to note that the Polynesian natives of *Aotearoa,* New Zealand have similar Indo-Aryan facial features to most Persians and as a suggestion perhaps a further DNA test should be carried out with Polynesian Maori and the people of Iraq and Iran? 2, 8, 30, 31, 43.

Question?
If Indo-Aryans came directly down from Mongolia to move eastwards into Asia as mentioned above, then the similarities between Egyptian culture and the Semitic language for Maori and Polynesians wouldn't be possible. Nevertheless, our research suggests there was at some point in time contact with the Ancient Egyptians, as all the evidence that we have come up with seems to point this out. This to us is more probable than other written works to date; moreover, it brings out the realistic nature of Biblical scripture in detail knowing that at some stage our Polynesian race had connections with the ancient Egyptians and Hebrew people.

Aramaic/Semitic language:
The ancient Semitic language (believed to be derived from Shem, the son of Noah), covered a wide area of the Near and Middle East that took in *Egyptian, Hebrew, Maltese, Libyan, Iraqi, Iranian, Syrian,* and *Tamil/Indian;* in other words a Universal Dialect although likeness to the Polynesian tongue changed depending where each of the tribal communities lived. It was this that the writer found so intriguing that it started his personal research back in the early 1960s. Gen: 11; 1. *View; Tower of Babel, from Wikipedia, free encyclopedia, (online).*

New Update:

The following information was presented to me in the form of photocopies whilst at the close of writing this particular paper/essay, and I have to admit that I found it intriguing and somewhat exciting. It was put together by the late Professor Barry Fells, from *'The Occasional Publications of the Epigraphic Society'* based in the United States of America, who was then an expert in the field of ancient migrations of the Near/Middle East, Indian and Pacific Oceans. To follow up on these findings the reader should check under *'Maurian, Libyan, and Egyptian'* using all three together on their computer screen. This will lead to a vast amount of material to follow through with as it provides detailed information of different cultures throughout the Pacific, also the discovery of at least 1000 ancient *text script/steles sites* covering the ancient sea-trade routes starting from an Egyptian, Libyan source that sailed around the continent of Africa where they traded in precious metals, spices, and silk in the times of the ancient Pharaohs.

'From Ezion-Geber, near Akaba, Israel's King Solomon's ships sailed down the Red Sea and returned from Arabia and Ethiopia loaded with gold.'

King Solomon, as taken from Biblical scripture, dated from 970 – 931 BCE, and if this holds true then Solomon's ships were trading in the Indian Ocean at least 2,980 years ago. Nevertheless, Professor Fells points out that there were Egyptian settlements in Java with the traders being of *Libyan* descent, referring to an ancient Maurian script (*written word*) using a Polynesian speaking type of dialect from ancient *Egypt* that left a trail of inscriptions spreading from *Oran* in the Near/Middle East, to include *Madagascar, Easter Island* and the *Americas*.
Furthermore, there is written and actual photographic evidence of boomerangs found in the child King of Tutankhamen Royal Egyptian

tomb thus giving evidence of contact, perhaps mining, in ancient *Sahul*/Australia. 7, 8, 30, 43. *(Online)*.

Hawk, (Kahu):
In the book called *'Trail Of The Hawk'*, the author Dr Cornelius van Dorp from Kaitaia in Northland, New Zealand with others moved and lived amongst the indigenous Indians of the Americas as part of their personal research. His book tells of the Hopi Indian lifestyle and their belief that a gathering of a white skinned people (Celtic) called the Water Clan came on boats across the waters. *(See paintings by artist George Catlin of white skinned Indians, Choctaw, stick ball game online).* The reader will be as amazed as we were with the following chant as its well known to most New Zealanders, based on the original Ancient Maurian Script: 30, 31.

'Hymn to the Risen Sun'
Ka-ma-te, Ka-m-te, ka-i Ra, Ka-i Ra;
Ka-ma-te, ka-ma-te, ka-i Ra, ka-i Ra;
Te-ne ta-nu-ta; pa ha-ru, pa ha-ru,
Na na-ne ti-ka ma-i, Sa-ka fi-te-te Ra;
Hu-pa-ne; Ka, hu-pa-ne, fi-te-te Ra;

Translation
It is fulfilled, it is fulfilled, Ra has risen, Ra has risen;
It is fulfilled, it is fulfilled, Ra has risen, Ra has risen;
This is the Resurrection from the dead. Ascending, ascending,
From the abyss. Give light to us. Cause the sun to rise,
To rise up; To shine; Rise up, leap up O Ra.

The Haka in Maori
Ka-ma-te! Ka-ma-te! Ka-ora! Ka-ora!
Ka-ma-te! Ka-ma-te! Ka-ora! Ka-ora!
Te-nei te-tanga-ta; pa hu-ru huru
Na na–ne ti-ki ma-i, Whaka-whiti-te Ra!
U-pa-ne! Ka, u-pa-na! Hu-pana! Kau-pane
Whiti -Te -Ra! Hi!

Translation
It is death! It is death! It is life! It is life!
It is death! It is death! It is life! It is life!
We're going to die! We're going to die!
We're going to live! We're going to live!
This is the man so hairy, who fetched,
And made the shine the sun!
Together! Keep together!
Up the step! A second step!
Out comes the sun! Ahh!

The above translation is Ngati Porou; other variations depend on where each iwi/tribes lives.

Who are the True Indigenous People of New Zealand?
Key word here is; **Indigenous:**
The Oxford Dictionary states the following;
'Of people who are born within a country, a native of the land.'
The English Thesaurus mentions;
'An aboriginal, home–grown, inborn, inherent native.'

An example:
When my family arrived at Pearsons International Airport, Toronto, Canada in 1990, not being natives of that land, we found our passports stamped as *'Landed Aliens', (Tautangata).*

My great-great-grandparents from the McLeod Clan came from the east coast of Nova Scotia in Canada via St Anne near Sydney on a sailing ship called the *Ellen Lewis,* landing at Auckland New Zealand on 11th May, 1860. If passports had been around then they also would have shown that they as immigrants would have been called *'Landed Aliens.'*

My family and I were born in this country and our government provided all with documentation as proof of citizenship as true natives of Aotearoa, whereas the McLeod family complete with child were Canadian citizens with documents to prove their nationality; they were Canadians, not natives of New Zealand, *'Landed Aliens.'*

<u>Worthy of note:</u>

Our great-great-grandmother's aunty was only a small child back then and before leaving Nova Scotia was given a gift by a *'Mi'kmaq* Indian' tribal Chieftain, a loyal dear family member who gave this child buckskin leather garments, complete with moccasins. This gift can still be viewed at the Waipu Stone Museum in a photograph taken of the passengers from the *Ellen Lewis* with a child wearing such clothing. Also the North American Indian costume, complete with moccasins, is still proudly displayed in a glass cabinet.

Today the New Zealand law as previously mentioned still applies explaining the difference between foreigners and the true natives of our country. This means that all those people regardless of race <u>who are born</u> in New Zealand are truly a native of *Aotearoa.* In other words we are all one people, one family *(Whanau),* a Pacific-multi-cultured society; 37, 54.

'He Iwi Tahi Tatou – We are one people'- All Kiwis.'

(*The name Kiwis derives from our national symbol of the kiwi, a flightless bird*).

Chapter Six:

The first People, Moriori, Waitaha (Children of Maui), Our Cultural Future, Maori today, Toronto, Utu/revenge/payback, A Nation Under Siege, Apartheid/segregation, A Massive Cover Up, Your Cooperation is required, Herea Te tangata ki Te whenua /Binding people to the land.

<u>The First People:</u>
According to the late Michael King the approximate date of arrival of Moriori into New Zealand was 1056 BP. King mentions that compared to Maori, the native Moriori had different facial features and culture.

* The *Moriori/Maru-iwi/Nga -iwi* had a dark skin, perhaps from an *African/Indian/Melanesian descent?*
* They never tattooed themselves.
* Always half buried their dead in sand, in a crouched sitting position looking out to sea.
* Used a different way to celebrate manhood than the former.
* Developed birth control methods.
* Wood carvings, murals and canoes were of different material and design.
* Overcame the need to take a life, thus being above those of a lower culture.
* They wore flax matting type material around the waist somewhat like the people from the Kingdom of Tonga in respect for their Queen/King.

The only thing in common to Maori would have to be the *hongi* nose greeting (*exchange of breath*), and language is slightly similar; in fact all of Polynesia shows a smattering of Middle Eastern Semitic tongue as mentioned above. 5, 18. *(See Genesis 11: 5-8).*

Waitaha (Children of Maui):
The actual date of arrival of the *Waitaha* into New Zealand is unknown, but it is presumed to be around 975 BCE - that's 2,986 BP. Most of the findings are as previously stated; they had dwellings of stone, man-made tunnels (hideaways) especially around the Rotorua lakes district, obtained the knowledge of greenstone manufacture, practiced successfully in aquaculture, horticulture, oceanography, psychology, astronomy, biology, herbal remedies, were highly skilled as carvers of stone, and manufacturers of fire-hardened wood and flax-fibre fishnets. All this knowledge was passed on to Maori.

Whilst in Northland, Sylvia and I approached the *Kaikohe 'Wananga School of Learning'*, and learnt of their views regarding the false Maori settlement claims that tell of their plight and fight for justice because of the hatred and prejudice being fabricated over land claims of different Maori *hapu* (sub tribes), that have created for themselves recent histories at the expense of the First Nations People. Could it be that the *Waitaha* originally came from an Indo-Aryan-Celtic descent?

'We looked like 'Uru kehu' with our hazel eyes, pale skin, red/fair hair. We were different.'

As the first people to settle *Aotearoa,* we asked, did your people build the famous *Kaimanawa* Stone Wall? Their reply; *"We didn't build it; it must have been from those who settled here before we arrived."*
In fact two books called *'Song of the Waitaha'* and *'Whispers of the Waitaha'* tell of their history as a people, colourfully and superbly put together as a learning tool for all. 4, 44 *View; waitaha.org.nz*

'What is important to our people is that the 'Waitaha' are the first people in our islands.'
Tipene O'Regan (Waitangi Tribunal.)

Our Cultural Future:
All the above findings are factual. The old history and the past negative differences between all cultures must be set aside. Today we are in a different millennium, a new age, a time for forgiveness, a new beginning, an *'Alpha'* if you like or a *'New World Order'* that we as New Zealanders all must share. The old *'Treaty of Waitangi'* has now been put aside and our Government has adopted another revised version now called the *Waitangi Tribunal'* (1975) especially designed for *Maori and Pakeha* by the *Crown* in such a way that both sides must agree on what ever issues are brought forward on certain rights by either race. 15, 33, 34, 36, 37, 54.

Worthy of note:
It is also interesting to note that the statistics of bloodlines between Maori and *Pakeha* (European) also stopped in 1975, *why?*

Maori today:
One must also remember due to the broad mixtures of cultural relationships within Aotearoa the pure blooded Maori as a race has now finally gone. At the signing of the *'Treaty'* in 1840 the population of New Zealand was as follows;
(1) The native population totaled 40,000 and over half were mixed blood, Pakeha-Maori.

(2) The number of Europeans settlers was only 2,050.

According to statistics as at 12.00pm, 13th March 2010, only 15% of Pakeha-Maori are left compared with New Zealand's total population of 4,358 464 million. From those figures there are 565,329 ethnic people usually living in New Zealand who *identify themselves* as Pakeha - Maori, of these only 84% live in the North Island whilst 13% live in the South. The rest are elsewhere.

Other indigenous races of the Pacific hold the view that the cut-off point given to tribal members is 50% pure blood, meaning they who hold less at 49% genes are no longer considered to be pure and are encouraged to move on, leave their tribe. (More on this later).19. 22, 36, 37.

When Cook arrived in New Zealand in 1769 the French were nearby with the view of claiming *Aotearoa* for themselves. A short time later the whalers and sealers arrived; due to their success other nationalities also joined the hunt. Historians tell us that sealers were often abandoned by their ships to carry on culling ashore for long periods before retrieving; in most cases those left behind took in Maori women as wives. Also the Bay of Islands became a hot spot for these sailors having relations with native women. Even some Maori chieftains offered or forced their wives and daughters onto sailors just to obtain muskets. After seventy one years of interbreeding half the native population had been recorded as Pakeha-Maori. 37, 54.

Question:
How many generations would it take for the changeover, knowing that the average lifespan of Polynesian Maori back then was recorded as being 35-40 years?

The crew onboard whaling ships ranged from Asian, African, South American, English, French, Scandinavian, Pacific Islanders and Russian seaman, thus Maori today will have an abundance of blood groups within their veins, one only has to look around the marae today to see the differences in skin tone, hair colour, eyes and facial features. Nevertheless, the relations between sailors and Maori women folk brought sexual diseases along with chickenpox and measles plus the common cold and influenza, thus reducing numbers even more. For example; the ships visiting Aotearoa since its discovery in 1769 were recorded as follows:

1769. (British) *Endeavour.*
1769. (French) *Mascarin & Macquis de Castris.*
1773. (British) *Resolution & Adventure.*
1777. (British) *Resolution & Discovery.*
1791. (British) *Discovery, Chatham & William & Ann.*
1792. (British) *HMS. Gorgon.*
1793. (French) *Recherché & Esperance.*
1793. (Spanish) *Descubierta & Atrevida.*
1793. (British) *Britannia & Daedulus.*
1814. (British) *Active.*
1820. (Russian) *Vostok & Mirnyy.*
1824. (French) *Coquille, Astrolabe, la Favorite & Zelee.*
1835. (British) *Beagle.*
1791- 1840 The Pacific Whaling Fleet numbered <u>760 ships</u> (too numerous to mention here) with a mixture of nationalities, which used *Aotearoa* as their base to offload cargo and supplies more than once.

<u>Authors note:</u>
The first Polynesian inhabitants I've called Polynesian-Maori whilst the second as Pakeha-Maori the latter taken from the time of the signing of the Treaty of Waitangi in 1840 due to the native population being half European decent.

<u>Toronto:</u> 'The meeting place,' (O*jibwa, Chippewa Indian – where the rivers meet*).

Whilst working at the 'Eaton Center' in downtown Toronto, I met a fellow Kiwi named John who owned an upscale gentleman's department store called 'Steels' where men's shirts, socks, ties, suits, and coats were all high quality apparel priced well above the norm. I was introduced to John over a luncheon; found that he was tall, broad shouldered, well spoken, dressed in a businessman's attire, an impressive young man in fact. I personally liked him the moment we met and continued to do so but what really took me by surprise; he was Maori. John's first question to me was; "Are they still handing out welfare *'Dole'* to my people?" My reply, "Yes." John then told us that it was wrong, it has to stop. He continued by telling Robert my manager and me his reasons.

He'd come to Canada after leaving a small township called *Moerewa*, near *Kawakawa* in Northland, New Zealand. As a young lad John tried everything to avoid school. Truancy didn't go down well with the education department or the local authorities, but he did what some young school kids did; abused the system and his education. It seems John's father worked at the local abattoirs/slaughterhouse where, as told by the local *Whanau* (extended family), John was promised employment at the 'Works' once he left school. It turns out that his father met with an accident that caused his death and after a period of time John's mother met and married a Canadian and moved to their new home in Toronto with John in tow.

Upon arrival in Ontario his stepfather and mother talked to John about his future, especially his education. To reinforce the message his folks drove him through and around the city parks, back streets, wherever there were bag ladies/men, drug addicts, drunkards, dope dealers, hookers etc. In the parks John saw people with supermarket trolleys loaded with junk, people lying down on benches with just a plastic bag or newspaper for shelter and warmth. Those unfortunates had absolutely nothing and yet somehow existed with little clothing and food scraps from wherever, mainly from garbage bins.

Returning home, John's stepfather was blunt and to the point. 'In Canada there is no such thing as the welfare system like in New Zealand, no handouts whatsoever'. His stepfather continued by telling him that his writing, speech, manners, in fact his whole education, were totally unacceptable if he wanted to live in Canada. John was given a choice right there and then to either shape up or get out and join the unfortunate few. This terrified John and over the next few years his folks stood by him, arranging tuition after High School, in weekends wherever, in fact whenever there was a free moment one would find John studying always looking for ways to improve himself, this continued through College/University.

When I met John in 1990 he had a master's degree and a sound business in one of the biggest and finest shopping malls in Canada. *(View; torontoeatoncentre.com).*

This message applies to all cultures within New Zealand having the same education as Pakeha (European,) with guidance, if astute enough; they will succeed in whatever field they choose.

Utu/Revenge/Vendetta/Pay back:
Unfortunately some Maori still hold past grievances against other *iwi* (tribes). We met a young lady at the Auckland Hospital who tearfully told us that her recent wedding had been a complete disaster. It seems that her husband had invited his *Whanau* (extended family) from the Waikato area and she did the same from the Taranaki district, with the end result that only five family members turned up. *Why?* The disputes that occurred during the Maori Wars (1820s) happened hundreds of years ago and it's this type of attitude that Maori must set aside, to be forgotten if we are to be as one people. Obviously problems such as this will have to be worked on especially tribal differences, changing their attitude towards all cultures in a positive way to benefit all parties. 'Utu-

Pay-back/revenge' is a Melanesian custom. 36, 37, 38, 39, 48, 54. *(Melanesian custom # eight).*

'The old tribal boundaries are now of historic interest only. We need a new sense of nationalism if we are to deal with our problems.' Sir Peter Tapsell.

'A Nation under Siege'
Apartheid, segregation:
Our government knows all about our pre-Maori history and due to the lack of foresight has bent over backwards to please one particular race at a tremendous cost to its citizens, with one tribe being paid nine times for the same terra firma. In doing so, without realizing, they have introduced segregation, due to compensation towards land and foreshore rights. This has encouraged greed and disputes, especially with our young and not so young radicals wanting to take control. Such foolishness has already led to bloodshed with properties destroyed, even threats and assaults to holiday makers wanting to camp over, land owners wanting build on their own private properties and not being allowed to, even to the extent of not allowing trampers into National Parks, a public property. We all have seen TV news and read the media items to know that all the above is true and as a combined body of New Zealanders we all must work together towards a better peaceful solution. 15, 36, 37, 54.

'If people cannot let go of their hatred of their enemies, they risk sowing the seeds of hatred among themselves.' President Clinton. *47.*

A Massive Cover Up?
It has been widely accepted that the first Europeans to New Zealand created atrocities against Maori who had been deprived of much of their land and because of this sought compensation. But for this to

happen there had to be full co-operation of government ministers, Maori leadership and perhaps university academics to put together a strategy designed to defame or debunk others who would try and prove otherwise.
When this happened a huge infrastructure developed to cope with the sudden number of treaty claims involving hundreds of millions of dollars of *public funds* firstly used to help *iwi* for legal fees then to honour the claims.

If one analyses the large sums of money the whole scenario becomes financially serious and many groups of people from different background and other organizations become involved, lives change, a new rich list is created, conspiracies are born and one or two are protecting their new-found investments whilst other Pakeha-Maori having great expectations are sadly still waiting after thirty-six years, and with Maori assets at **$36 billion NZD.** Why? 54. View *'New Zealand in Crisis'* (online).

The risk of corruption within becomes very real and is evident by a governmental enquiry that investigated New Zealand solicitors. It now can be established that these treaty claims have already opened the way for opportunists and corruption on both sides. This happened in December 2009 and the New Zealand government appointee at the time was Dame Margaret Bazley - she had been slating this profession. *

We also have to assume at the time of the compensation that both Government and *iwi* had the best intentions to settle land claims as quickly as possible, however the press and general outcry from the public was **'One Country, One Nation, One People'** but this can never happen whilst there are so many outstanding land claims by Maori.

This last statement is a very complex issue as it includes *'Tanga Whenua'* (first people of the land), and now that it has been proved that Maori were definitely not the first people here, it will have the potential of creating enormous racial conflict within New Zealand. Maori would lose much of their pride (*mana*) making many of their leaders look dishonest. 36, 37, 54. * Paloma Migone' report for NZPA, Friday 27th November, 2009 (online).

Mana: Man, Self-esteem, an honour, self-importance, supernatural or a presence, to some a gift.
Manna: As taken from a Semitic/Middle Eastern dialect with the same meaning as above.

Your co-operation is required:
The whole nation of New Zealand must come together 'as one people' but this time to involve all cultures, not just Maori. To do this we must include governmental ministers regardless of which party they belong to who must put aside their political differences, to come forth collectively with one accord, to transform our country into a *multicultural nation* with a future, a relationship that needs to be built on trust thus giving a sense of belonging, something tangible that all our cultures can be proud of. A *bi-cultural* government with just two races will simply not work. As proven throughout history, it has to be a combined effort including all our cultures.15, 40.

Herea Te tangata ki Te whenua: 'Binding the people to the land:'
It's a universal world we live in; nobody owns a country. This is unwritten 'Universal Lore'; we are all caretakers. The most important thing in this world isn't land; *it is people especially our children.* Not just dollars and cents, nor political votes; no matter what culture, it is they who are our future.

In my youth I found the local Maori a proud fun loving people who had stood alongside other Kiwi Europeans *(Pakeha)* fighting the same enemy throughout both 1st and 2nd World Wars and sadly some never returned. The New Zealand Maori Battalion, being natural warriors, saw it as their duty to fight just as other *'Kiwis'* did who loved *Aotearoa, 'Land of The White Long Cloud,'* a nation of mixed diverse ethnic cultures.

'We are one house and if our Pakeha brothers fall, we also fall with them.' Sir Apirana Ngata, 1940.'

Chapter Seven:

Wake up New Zealand, A country that's divided will fall, The message, A National Day of Prayer, Incident # One, Incident # Two, A No Win Situation, Conclusion, Epilogue, A Spiritual Awareness, New Zealand's National Anthem, Bibliography, References & Further Reading, Post Script, The Challenge, Manual for all mankind.

<u>Wake up New Zealand:</u>
We must come together <u>as one,</u> in a *hui* (gathering) or whatever, where *all cultures* can partake without violence or any words spoken in anger. We have failed miserably to provide a vision to our society that gives a sense of wanting to belong. The present system has to change if we want to progress, by having the same set of rules for all, not one for Pakeha and another for Maori. This time we need equal opportunities for all, a much improved educational system, one law, one flag, one coalition government, having joint interests with the hope of fostering mutual trust and understanding <u>involving all our cultures,</u> and lastly let's do away with the one-sided corrupt *'Waitangi Tribunal'* to bring back the original *'Treaty of Waitangi'* in its original form as it was so designed, protecting <u>all New Zealanders</u> and not just Maori.

<u>Worthy of note:</u>
All new Zealanders, irrespective of race, colour or creed should be extremely concerned about a new constitution. 54. *View: 'New Zealand in Crisis' (online).*

"Impossible," some ministers will say, but it's been done before and can be done again, this time using the right people. It's a matter of restructuring, knowing who and how to do it. To avoid conflict we all must get our act together **NOW,** otherwise we will be like those other unfortunate countries, ending up with lawlessness and bloodshed simply because their cultural relationships were ignored, left too late to solve the nation's problems, in fact this is history repeating itself over *'land issues',* the main cause of the past Maori tribal wars. The same happened in Central and South America, South Africa, Uganda, Congo, Eastern Europe, Afghanistan, Iraq, Iran, India, Pakistan, Israel, Palestine and Cuba, and the unrest continues to happen in Syria, Libya, Egypt, Greece, Italy and in the United States. Must we add New Zealand to this list? 4, 15, 34, 36, 37, 40, 44, 47, 48. 34, 37, 54. *View: 'Robbery by Deceit' (Online).*

'It is my prayer to my God above that we will all learn to live as one people in New Zealand, the Maori and the Pakeha, living together as one nation.' **Dame Whina Cooper M.B.E. C.B.E.**

<u>*'A country that's divided will fall,'*</u> (Luke 11: 17).
Some readers may think that we are over reacting and the above isn't true. Others may think that we are vindicated racists; we certainly are not so, we are a peaceful loving Kiwi couple who are **'*realists'*** and deeply concerned for our cultures and the welfare of our country. It seems that most Kiwis lead a very sheltered life, or perhaps know about the above issues and hope the problem will just go away? In reality there is conflict between our different cultures taking place even now whilst you read this. The hatred towards Pakeha and Maori alike by activists on both sides is unbelievable, as if an evil presence or spiritual warfare were taking place. There are some violent young men and women amongst us who just want to take control, but they must realize that violence is the pleasure of fools and the last resort of wise men.

'Violence is the last refuge of the incompetent'. Isaac Asimov.

The Message:
What we really need is a 'Spiritual Renewal' in this country. Why? (a) Because, one cannot use weapons of mass destruction against spiritual forces of darkness. (b) I seriously doubt if New Zealand is going to exist another generation without bloodshed unless we turn our attention back to Christ, if we don't have a turning towards religion in this country.

'If my people, which are called by my name, shall humble themselves, and pray, and seek my face, and turn from their wicked ways; then will I hear from Heaven, and will forgive their sin, and will heal their land'
2nd Chronicles 7: 14 (KJV).

What we need in New Zealand is a **'National Day of Prayer'** intercession for a divine intervention. Our society cannot exist without a judge or a referee to sort the difference between good and evil. Without guidelines, support and suppression we will return to the old habits of an uncivilized quality of life as some cultures have done. Science has not the standards to choose from right or wrong, nor has politics. Only an acceptable set of principles can do this, and our democratic way of biblical standards has been encouraged and sanctified by the name of religion. I am deeply supportive of the solid work the church does in helping to structure our society. If anything we must bind together as one people for the good of this country and not in destructive discord. We must work as a team to blend in with our different cultures. If we separate, we will destroy ourselves. If we work in with each other, we can create a wonderful way of life for all.

When I was a young man I used to think how lucky we were compared with other countries. When you think about it we have fine beaches, healthy clean air, abundance of food resources, great outdoors and tramping in our alpine mountains, hot mineral springs, a warm temperate climate, the best of camping, boating, fishing and sailing waters around the Sounds of the South Island, Auckland's Hauraki Gulf and the Bay of Islands in the far north. In fact we were known back then as a Pacific Island Paradise, showing the rest of the world how to really live. It wasn't so long ago in the mid-seventies that New Zealand was voted the third best country in the world, but how things have changed. What happened; where did we go so terribly wrong?

Today we have separatism, a racial problem brought on by political blundering, so much so that the native born New Zealanders within this country are now really upset for good reason. *Why?* In fact I'll give you a couple of examples of a lesser kind; the first was a mother who should have had the patience to listen first before speaking out. The second was due to a young radical *Pakeha-Maori* not getting his facts right first, who took matters into his own hands.

Incident # One 2002:

We were in the public domain of *Opito Bay* near Kerikeri in the Bay of Islands collecting our mail, and after having coffee that morning we returned to find my dinghy missing. It turned out that a young Pakeha-Maori lad of high school age was using it so I attracted his attention and waved him to the shore. Upon his arrival I suggested that I didn't mind him rowing around in my dinghy, but he should at least have had the manners to ask me first. Whereupon his mother, who was sitting in the family vehicle, heard our conversation and yelled out for all to hear, **"It's on our land."** *(Is this the beginning of foreshore rights?)*

Incident # Two 2004:

This happened in *Wharangaere/Crater Bay* in Tepuna Inlet in the Bay of Islands. Sylvia and I were on our vessels *Murihiku* and *Haumoana* catching up with maintenance; this we have done each year within the same inlet. We had been there for two days just doing our thing when out of the blue arrived a tinny about 18ft in length complete with a cuddy cabin, towing two teenagers in a doughnut. This 'Fish-o' vessel named *'Catch Up'* came extremely close, within 10ft, at high speed. At the helm was a young Pakeha-Maori chap aged at a guess in his late twenties who should have known better. His motives were deliberate and dangerous as he sped between both vessels still towing those kids. When challenged as to why he was doing this his reply was very clear, **"Get the F... out of our bay you F... Pakeha, it's our F...bay, our F...fish, our F...waters etc,"**

In due course this foul mouthed tinny driver returned to the southern entrance of Crater Bay where there were tents of different sizes erected, obviously visitors to the region that must be known to the local Maori settlement nearby. A call over the VHF marine radio to the local Harbour Master and Coastguard didn't help our situation at all; we were told to leave the area to avoid conflict as there was nothing they could do. Reluctantly we finally raised our anchors and returned to our moorings in Opito Bay.

We have since have heard of the same conduct towards others within the same area, one being an overseas cruising vessel. It makes me wonder at times what tales those visitors passed on in emails back home thus discouraging other travellers. It's this type of attitude that makes us feel ashamed of our personal connections within Maoridom.

A no-win situation:
When you have suppression there will be resentment
And when you have resentment there will be resistance
And when you have resistance there will be violence
And when you have violence there will be suppression,
And when you have suppression...

Conclusion:
Our Cultural Differences:
The writer is a native of Aotearoa from a mixture of cultures; likewise, Sylvia my partner is also a New Zealander, definitely not Maori, as her family is from a Spanish/South American origin. Her great-grandfather Emanuel (the baker) was a Chilean and sailed out to New Zealand in a whaling ship from Valparaiso.

My late father's family was of Celtic, French and Scandinavian heritage and his mother was from gypsy/Hebrew stock. Moreover, my late mother's background is surprisingly different from the above, having sea-faring Highlanders as from a family of McLeod's, mostly farmers and some builders of sailing ships, originally from Scotland then from St Anne's in Nova Scotia, Canada, as mentioned beforehand, that sailed to Waipu, New Zealand. Strange as it may seem, my wife's family the 'Stewarts', also of Scottish descent, arrived in New Zealand on the same *Ellen Lewis* as my family the 'McLeod's from Nova Scotia.

I'm supposed to have *Mi'kmaq* Native Indian blood within my veins; but regardless of the blood grouping it doesn't mean I'm Maori, North American Indian, Jewish, nor a Scottish Highlander. My heritage actually states that I'm a genuine native, a Kiwi-born New Zealander.

Today, whatever the gene percentage, it's identical to our <u>diverse</u> Pakeha-Maori having the same; the fact is we are all one people, a *multi-cultural-coloured society* from different nationalities, a proud diverse Pacific Island Nation in the South Pacific.

The summation:

So there you have it, in a condensed form of our cultural differences; if it wasn't for the invention of computers, access to websites or e-books this essay in a printed book format would have been huge in volume.

We started this essay by checking out the past history of Melanesia, and found *Aotearoa* New Zealand to be already inhabited by Melanesians before a Polynesian-Maori settlement. Then whilst searching our family history we found a newspaper clipping taken from 'The Evening Post,' 29th March, 1926 regarding a navigational calabash sextant with another interesting find that covered early Melanesian fortifications and their settlements. The Antarctic Migration theory with the question; did the Australian Barrinean Pygmy and the Tasmanian Native really traverse the southern continent from Africa? Furthermore, the *Vaka* voyage sailing eastwards from Henderson Island to Peru in South America was shown by our research that such a journey against natural disadvantages simply wasn't possible. In addition and unbeknown to some readers, the ancient Semitic language from the Near/Middle East is surprisingly similar throughout Oceania depending on where one lives. Historians also mention that a movement of mixed cultures traversed the coastal regions from the Near/Middle East to finally sojourn in Asia then after a period of time left Austroasia by foot to traverse the Bering Strait to the Americas whilst others sailed towards the sun in open vessels identical in design from India always searching for a new home.

These folk were the explorers of 'The True Great Migration' having left their original *Hawaiki* a Mesopotamian homeland to traverse through Egypt and Libya approximately 2000 - 1,289 BCE and not from a Pacific Island as first believed. This new development opened the way for others taking in Papua New Guinea, Malaya, Java, Melanesia, Philippines, New Caledonia, Vanuatu, Fiji, Nui, Samoa, Tonga, Cooks,

Marquises, Tahiti, Rapa-nui, Hawaiian Islands, the Americas, the sub-Antarctic Auckland Islands and finally *Aotearoa* New Zealand. These were the early Polynesians, a race of mixed cultures who completed one of the greatest feats of exploration in history; a race of seafarers who made do with what they had just using the basic natural resources available.

Epilogue:
In 1931 the Australian Sir Grafton Elliot-Smith examined a mummified body found in a New Zealand cave and identified the skull as being that of an ancient Egyptian at least 2000 years old. His papers and finds have since been illegally removed. *Why?*

'Vikings of the Sun Rise:'
By Sir Peter Henry Buck 1877 – 1951 *(Te Rangihiroa)*, was first printed in 1938 and I'm pleased to say is still in its original form. However, *'The Coming of the Maori'* last published 1987 by the same author isn't the same book that I read whilst at college. *Why?*
The author's name is still on the cover but contents are not personally his, being completely revamped into a different modern text altogether. Nevertheless, on page seventy there is mention; *'a connection, evidence of an affinity between the Polynesian language and the Sanskrit from India,'* also *'there seems to be a connection with ancient Ur of the Chaldees.'*

'Ancient Celtic New Zealand:'
The book and disc has been illegally removed from some libraries along with 'The New Zealand Gazette' dated 1867. *Why? The former can be obtained online.* 4.

Highly recommended reading:
For Maori youth I suggest they read a fantastic true story written by Maori for Maori a *Mentor, an Eagle* that tells of how to be a success in life in a Pakeha (European) world. 24.

A Spiritual Awareness:
No one owns New Zealand - as with all countries, we are just caretakers. Being realistic they all belong to 'Him' the 'One True God of all Nations, known as the 'Creator of the Universe, the G-d of Abraham, Isaac and Jacob,' Yahweh/Elohim, 'Most High G-d, Ado-nai, Jehovah, El Shaddai, G-d Almighty, a **God of love** *(Aroha)* who is *the light of this world* there is no other as equal …period.'

Light of this world:
The light shines in the darkness, and the darkness has not suppressed it. This was the true light, which gives light to everyone entering the world. He was in the world – the world came to be through him – yet the world did not know him. He came to his own homeland, yet his own people did not receive him. 5.

Key word is Love:
In fact our own New Zealand National Anthem mentions *in the bonds **of love** we meet,* it's a togetherness, it's spiritual prayer asking God to defend our free land, we are all asking/seeking for **'His'** divine protection, the key word here again is **LOVE.** *(1. Corinthians: 13).*

New Zealand's National Anthem:

God of Nations at Thy feet,
In the bonds of **love** we meet,
Hear our voices we entreat,
God defend our free land.
Guard Pacific triple star,
From the shafts of strife and war,
Make her praises heard afar,
God defend New Zealand.

Men of every creed and race,
Gather here before Thy face,
Asking Thee to bless this place,
God defend our free land.
From dissention, envy, hate,
And corruption guard our State,
Make our country good and great
God defend New Zealand.

Peace, not war, shall be our boast,
But, should foe assail our coast,
Make us then a mighty host,
God defend our free land.
Lord of battles in Thy might,
Put our enemies to flight,
Let our cause be just and right,
God defend New Zealand.

Let our **love** for Thee increase,
May Thy blessings never cease,

Give us plenty, give us peace,
God defend our free land.
From dishonour and from shame,
Guard our country's spotless name,
Crown her with immortal fame,
God defend New Zealand.

May our mountains ever be,
Freedom's ramparts on the sea,
Make us faithful unto Thee,
God defend our free land.
Guide her in the nation's van,
Preaching **love** and truth to man,
Working out Thy glorious plan,
God defend New Zealand.

ONE NATION

'He Iwi Tahi Tatou – We are one people- all Kiwis.'

A proud multicultural island nation

In the far reaches of the Southern Pacific.

Aotearoa – New Zealand

This land is my land this land is your land
From Cape Reinga to the Stewart Island,
From the kauri forests to the sparkling waters,
This land was made for you and me.
(Gisborne Folk Club)

Honore & Matauranga (Honour & Wisdom).

o0o

THE END

Bibliography:

References & Further Reading:

(1) New Zealand, Fiji & Vanuatu Museums.

(2) 'The Story of Old Wairoa, East Coast, North Island, New Zealand,' by contributing authors Sir Tiri Carol, Sir Peter Buck, & Thomas Lambert etc.

(3) 'Vikings of the Sunrise & the Coming of the Maori.' by Sir Peter Buck (Te Rangi Hiroa.)
Published by Coulls, Summerville, Wilkie, in Dunedin in New Zealand.

(4) 'Ancient Celtic New Zealand' by Martin Dout'e *(www.celticnz.co.nz)*.

(5) 'Ancient Lands of the Bible' by Readers Digest, the 'King James Bible' & 'Jewish Torah or Download an electronic e-Pentateuch, e-sword or e-bible' for Scripture references. *(Online)*'

(6) '1421. The Year China Discovered the World,' from the book by Gavin Menzies R.N. ISBN 978–0-553-81522-1*(Online)*.

(7) Pre - Tasman Explorers by Ross M. Wiseman. ISBN 0-473-04505-2.

(8) Ancient Iraq by Georges Roux. ISBN0-14-020828-3.

(9) The Manila Galleon, Lytle Schurz 1939.

(10) By William Re – Polynesian Society, Vol. 37, No 4 pages 367-368, (December 1928.
Contributor; Edward Harding). *(Online)*.

(11) *www.zealand.org.nz/new_zealand.htm*

(12) *www.1421.tv/pages/evidence/content.asp? Evidence ID=295*

(13) *www.celticnz.co.nz/embargo_saga.html*

(14) *www.morien-institute.org*

(15) 'Robbery by Deceit'/'Billion Dollar Rip off of God's Own' By Allan Titford. *(Online)*.

(16) Pioneering Reminiscences of Old Wairoa, by T Lambert. Published by Thomas Avery & Sons Ltd, New Plymouth, in 1936, New Zealand.

(17) History of New Zealand, by Mike King. ISBN0 143018671.

(18) Moriori; A People Rediscovered, Mike King. Waitangi Massacre ISBN 0670826553.

(19) The Quest for Origins, by K R Howe, ISBN 0143018574.

(20) Vaka Moana Voyages of the Ancestors by K R Howe BSBN-13; 978-1-83953-625-1.

Also BSBN 10; 1-86953-625-8. *(Online).*

(21) The Spanish Discovery of New Zealand, by Ross Wiseman, ISBN 0-473-03883-8.

(22) Come Onshore and We Will Kill you and Eat You All, by Christina Thompson, a Dooms Bury Publication, ISBN 978 0 7475 9815 2.

(23) Last of the whalers, by Heather Heberley, ISBN 0-90856-90-3.

(24) Ancient Wisdom Modern Solutions, by Ngahihi O Te Ra Bidois, ISBN 978-0-473-15060-0.

(25) Maori Peoples of New Zealand, ISBN-13:978-1-86953-622-0. *(Online).*

(26) New Zealand Mysteries, by Robyn Jenkins, ISBN 0 589 00494 8.

(27) Man on the Rim, by Alan Thorne & Robert Raymond. ISBN 0 207 16246 8.

(28) We, the Navigators, by Dr David Lewis, ISBN 0 589 00 741 6.

(29) Daughters of the Wind, by Dr David Lewis, 1967.

(30) The Epigraphic Society, 6 Woodland St, Arlington, Mass, USA 02171. *(Online).*

(31) Trail of the Hawk, by Dr Cornelius van Dorp, ISBN 0-9597948-6-7.

(32) Landmarks, by Kenneth B Cumberland. ISBN O 909486 89 1.

(33) The People Before, by Gary Cook & Thomas Brown, published by Stove Print Press ISBN 0-582040-4. PP 148 – 150. *(Online).*

(34) Investigate Magazine, January 2004. *www.celticnz.org/TreatyBook/chapter07.htm (Online).*

(35) Maps of Ancient Sea Kings, by Charles Hapgood, Published by Adventures Unlimited Press, SBN 0932813429- 9780932813428, Amazon Books. *(Online).*

(36) History of New Zealand And Its Inhabitants, by Dom Felice Vaggioli, Published by the University of Otago Press, Dunedin, ISBN 1 877133 52 3.

(37) From Treaty To Conspiracy, by H R Baker, Published by One New Zealand Foundation Inc. Press 1998.ISBN O-473-05066-8. *(Online).*

(38) The Musket Wars, by RD Crosby, ISBN 0-7900-0677-4.

(39) Pakeha Maori, by Trevor Bentley, ISBN 0-14-028540-7.

(40) NGA TAMA TOA, The Price of Citizenship, C Company 28 (Maori) Battalion 1939-45. By Monty Soutar, Published by David Bateman Ltd, Albany, New Zealand.

(41) The Lunar Code, by Ken Ring, ISBN 13- 978186 941 8526, Random House Publications.

(42) Sea Routes to Polynesia, by Thor Heyerdahl, Published by Unwin Brothers Ltd, UK. 1968.

(43) Egypt Land of the Pharaohs, By Time Life books, ISBN: 1 84447 051 2.

(44) Song of the Waitaha, Whispers of the Waitaha by Barry Brailsford, *www.waitaha.org/*

(45) New Zealand and the South Pacific Islands, by John Chambers. A Windrush Press Book.

(46) The New Zealanders A Story of Austral Lands, Translated by Carol Legg 1992, Victoria Press
992. ISBN 0 86473 233 3.

(47) In the Name of Sorrow and Hope, Noa Ben Artzi- Pelossof, ISBN 0-8052-1084-9 Random House.com

(48) From Maui to Cook: The discovery & settlement of the Pacific. Dr David Lewis, ISBN 0 86824 00. Also ISBN 0 86824 002 8 Limited-ed. Doubleday Publications Australia Pty Ltd.

(49) 'Space' by James Albert Michener, Random House Publications NY 1982, ISBN 0436279673.

(50) The Billy Graham Story, by Billy Graham Evangelistic Association, ISBN: 0-310 25126-5.

(51) New Zealand: A Short History: Laurie Barber, Century Hutchinson New Zealand Ltd, ISBN 1 86941 0491.

(52) The Maori Pa: by Edison Best, Publisher Dominion Museum Bulletin # 6. Museum of New Zealand Te Papa, Tongarewa 1995. ISBN O - 909010-39-0. *View online*

(53) 'Journey of Man,' the Story of the Human Species, Hosted by Dr Spencer Wells, a PBS DVD Video Presentation.

(54) New Zealand in Crisis: by Ross Baker, One New Zealand Foundation, *View online.*

(55) Amiria; The Life Story of a Maori Woman, Amiria Manutahi Stirling as told by Anne Salmond, Published by AH & AW Reed; ISBN 058 009788.

Post Script:
'Sit down before fact as a child. Be prepared to give up every preconceived notion. Follow humbly where God leads you or you will learn nothing.'

The Challenge:
The Bible and Torah/Pentateuch/Tanakh (Heb) is an infallible guide for all ages; it's astonishingly prophetic. There is a mention about the close of an age when man will be lovers of pleasure, idol worshippers and researching heritages. Looking back seventy odd years the writer is able to affirm that it's all too true.

Is the Holy Scripture true or false?
Here are a few questions for you to check out whilst using your Bible/Pentateuch (Heb) and if you don't have a Bible you can download an electronic E-Bible, E-Sword, 'Bible Gateway' or 'Daily Bible Guide'.
The *Tanakh (Heb)* can also be found online, once opened check out below and then you decide…

Question:
How did Columbus know the world was round when mankind at the time thought the earth was flat?

*   The earth is rounding as told 2,700 years ago. *Yesha'yahu (Heb) Isaiah 40: 22.*

   'It is he that sitteth upon the circle of the earth, and the inhabitants thereof are as grasshoppers; that stretcheth out the heavens as a curtain, and spreadeth them out as a tent to dwell in:'

*   The Earth hangs on nothing but a void,' written 3000 years ago. *Iyov, (Heb) Job: 26; 7.*

'He stretcheth out the north over the empty place, and hangeth the earth upon nothing'.

*   That man certainly lived with dinosaurs. *Iyov, (Heb) Job: 40; 15-24. 41; 1-34.*

Chapter 40: 15-24.
'Behold now behemoth, which I made with thee; he eateth grass as an ox. 16. Low now, his strength is in his loins, and his force is in the navel of his belly. 17. He moveth his tail like a cedar; the sinews of his stones are wrapped together. 18. His bones as strong pieces of brass; His bones are like bars of iron. 19. He is the chief of the ways of God; he that made him can make his sword to approach unto him. 20. Surely the mountains bring him forth food, where all the beasts of the field play. 21. He lieth under the shady trees, in the covert of the reed, and ferns. 22. The shady trees cover him with their shadows; the willows of the brook compass him about. 23. Behold, he drinketh up a river, and hasteth not; he trusteth that he can draw up the Jordan into his mouth. 24. He taketh it with his eyes his nose pierceth through snares.'

Chapter 41: 1-34.
'Canst thou draw out leviathan with an hook? Or his tongue with a cord which thou lettest down? 2. Canst thou put an hook into his nose? Or bore his jaw through with a thorn? 3. Will he make many supplications unto thee? Will he speak soft words unto thee? 4. Will he make a covenant thee? Wilt thou take him for a servant for ever? 5. Wilt thou play with him as with a bird? Or wilt thou bind him for thy maidens? 6.

Shall the companions make a banquet of him? Shall they part him amongst the merchants? 7. Canst thou fill his skin with barbed iron or his head with fish spears? 8. Lay thine hands upon him, remember the battle, do no more. 9. Behold, the hope of him is in vain: shall not one be cast down even at the sight of him? 10. None is so fierce that dare stir him up: who then is able to stand before me? 11. Who hath prevented me, that I should repay him? Whatsoever is under the whole of heaven is mine. 12. I will not conceal his parts, nor his power, nor his comely proportion. 13. Who can cover the face of his garment? Or who can come to him with his double bridle? 14. Who can open doors of his face? His teeth are terrible round about. 15. His scales are his pride, shut up together as with a close seal. 16. One is so near to another, that no air can come between them. 17. They are joined to one another, that they cannot be sundered. 18. By his nessings a light doth shine, and his eyes are like the eyelids of the morning. 19. Out of his mouth go burning lamps, and sparks of fire leap out. 20. Out of his nostrils goeth smoke, as out of a seething pot or caldron. 21. His breath kindleth coals, and a flame goeth out of his mouth. 22. In his neck remainth strength, and sorrow is turned to joy before him. 23. The flakes of his flesh are joined together: they are firm in themselves; they cannot be moved. 24. His heart is as firm as stone; yea, as hard as a piece of the nether millstone. 25. When he rises up himself, the mighty are afraid: by reason of breakings they purify themselves. 26. The sword of him that layeth at him cannot hold: the spear, the dart, nor the habergeon. 27. He asteemeth iron as straw, and brass as rotten wood. 28. The arrow cannot make him flee: slingstone are turned with him into stubble. 29. Darts are counted as stubble: he laugheth at the shaking of a spear. 30. Sharp stones are under him: he spreadeth sharp pointed things upon the mire. 31. He maketh the deep to boil like a pot: he maketh the sea like a pot of ointment. 32. He maketh a path to shine after him; one would think the deep to be hoary. 33. Upon the earth there is not his like, who is made without fear. 34. He beholdeth all high things; he is king over all the children of pride.' <u>*View; Jurassic art & Evolution.fact.org (Online).*</u>

Water in outer space:
H2o is a gas in liquid form most of which is found in the vastness of outer space; water that's solid ice some in the shape and as large of our own planet as found around our galaxy systems. For example, the rings of our planet Saturn are made of ice, some pieces as large as railroad coaches whilst others are as small as ice cubes. Comets are made of ice, some are as large as mountains; they are a carrier of life forms in suspended hibernation encased within; this amazing discovery was only found within the last decade, yet was foretold thousands of years ago.

It is also interesting to note when looking at an Atlas of Central America one can see the rounding shape of the Caribbean inner sea with a host of islands at the edge. This rounding was formed by the impact of a large comet; another formed Hudson Bay in the Canadian wilderness and yet another impact was in the Indian Ocean near the Ganges River delta. <u>*View: shoemaker-levy 9 (online).*</u>

'A Manual' for mankind:
The *Bible, Torah/Pentateuch* (Heb) takes in all the problems that our planet offers today and in return gives wisdom on how to correct them, some of which are as follows; human conduct, resourcefulness, finances, health & spiritual wellness issues, farming, technical input, law and order, personal hygiene, food preparation science, marine technology, technical construction of large and small complexes, governmental science, marriage/partnership and what to look for and avoid etcetera. In other words the scriptures should not to be taken lightly, they are definitely not foolishness.

I offer all believers and non-believers a challenge, read the scriptures in privacy away from scoffers, and whilst doing so take note of what it says about the above and your own personal future.

If you have a well developed loving heart
You are more likely to see the good in people,
Not letting it be camouflaged by their flaws.

Even if you are the minority of one, the truth is still the truth.
Mahatma Gandhi.

Disclaimer:
Opinions expressed in this book do not necessarily represent nor necessarily reflect those of various authors, editors and the owners of this work, consequently, parties mentioned or implied cannot be held liable or responsible for such opinions.

Copyrights: R.M. Bodle 2011:
Ross M. Bodle has the asserted right to be identified as author of this book/work.

All rights reserved:
No part of this publication (whether it be in any eBook, digital, electronic or traditionally printed format or otherwise) may be reproduced, except for the purpose of fair reviewing. It may not be stored in a retrieval system, or transmitted, in any form by any means, electronic, digital or mechanical, including CD, DVD, eBook, PDF format, photocopying, recording or any information storage and retrieval system, including by any means via the internet or World Wide Web, or by any means yet undiscovered, without the prior written permission of
the copywriter owners and the publisher of this book/work. Infringers of copyright render themselves liable to
prosecution.

See another book by this author, **Sea Gypsies Down Under.**

It contains actual experiences of cruising folk who share their stories of storms, shipwrecks, man-overboard, pirates & gunshot victims, diving experiences and shark attacks, with helpful advice passed on by those who have already been there.

Anybody who has dreamed of throwing off the shackles of everyday life and running away to sea will find this book invaluable. It paints a true picture of life on board – the highs and lows – and gives expert advice on avoiding the many pitfalls that novice sailors fall into.

With a foreword by Grant Dalton and interviews with Sir Peter Blake's crew on Seamaster, this book puts you among the sailing greats. Whether you're an armchair sailor or a real old salt, these interviews with genuine people living the dream will entertain and inspire you. Enjoy!

Available from Amazon in print and for Kindle, or Smashwords for all ebook formats.

Buy the print book here https://www.createspace.com/3847691
Buy the ebook here http://www.smashwords.com/books/view/116290